Michael Chiarello's

FLAVORED OILS and VINEGARS

Michael Chiarello's

FLAVORED OILS AND VINEGARS

100 Recipes for Cooking with Infused Oils and Vinegars

PHOTOGRAPHS BY Daniel Proctor

CHRONICLE BOOKS
SAN FRANCISCO

First Chronicle Books LLC paperback edition, published in 2006.

ISBN-10: 0-8118-5536-8
ISBN-13: 978-0-8118-5536-5

The Library of Congress has cataloged the previous editions as follows:

Chiarello, Michael.
    Flavored oils: 50 recipes for cooking with infused oils/
    by Michael Chiarello, with Penelope Wisner; photography by Daniel Proctor
        p. cm.
        Includes index.
        ISBN 0-8118-0898-X
        1. Cookery (Olive Oil) 2. Spices. I. Wisner, Penelope. II. Title
    TX819.O42C45   1995
    641.6'463—dc20   94-27961
                                    CIP
Chiarello, Michael.
    Flavored vinegars: 50 recipes for cooking with infused vinegars/
    by Michael Chiarello, with Penelope Wisner; photography by Daniel Proctor
        p. cm.
        Includes index.
        ISBN 0-8118-0872-6
        1. Cookery (Vinegar) 2. Vinegar. I. Wisner, Penelope. II. Title
    TX819.V5C45   1996
    641.6'2—dc20   95-21547
                                    CIP

Manufactured in China

DESIGNED BY **Lauren Criscione**

Distributed in Canada by Raincoast Books
9050 Shaughnessy Street
Vancouver, British Columbia V6P 6E5

10 9 8 7 6 5 4 3 2 1

Chronicle Books LLC
85 Second Street
San Francisco, California 94105

www.chroniclebooks.com

TABLE of CONTENTS

ACKNOWLEDGMENTS

Heartfelt thanks to my amazing family: to my adored wife and best bud, Eileen, who taught me what the flavor of life truly is. To Margaux, Felicia, and Giana, my three daughters, for their unrestrained love. To Aidan, my son. Welcome to the family. We all have anxiously awaited your joyous arrival.

Your journey begins.

When I think about all the people who deserve thanks for their participation in my career, for listening to my dreams and then pitching in to make them come true, the list gets very, very long. It all starts with my loving, passionate mother, Antoinette. Flavor was the currency she traded in.

I am glad to have the opportunity to give special thanks to a few more people: To Michael Laukaurt, my great friend and product partner of fifteen years for his total dedication, belief, and loyalty. He has spent countless hours preparing and bottling my food product ideas for three companies. Our friendship makes all we create together taste twice as good.

To my Food Network and Fine Living fans, thanks for getting me out of the hot restaurant kitchen and into the comfort of your homes each and every day. The ideas I present, which have served me well over the years, are for you. Please remember, if you start with great organic ingredients and finish with people at your table whom you care for, you will have a recipe for success each and every time.

Thanks go to my brother, Dr. Ronald Chiarello, for his very analytical perspective on the chemistry of vinegar making. Please send me the Cliffs Notes. To my mother-in-law, Judi, and father-in-law, Denis, thank you for being the best consumer-tasting panel we could ever dream of.

To my NapaStyle team, thank you for believing we could bring great flavor to every room of the house. The journey with you is our destination. To Darrel Corti, thanks for generously sharing your amazing knowledge of all that can be consumed. To Daniel Proctor, photographer, and Merilee Hague-Bordin, stylist, thanks for adding an entirely new dimension to my books. It has been very exciting to see my work transformed through Daniel's lens.

To my dear friend and cowriter, Penni Wisner, who makes my passion for sharing my love of food and cooking a tremendous joy. I am truly blessed to have crossed paths with her. Thank you, Penni!

To my friend and Chronicle Books editor, Bill LeBlond, a heartfelt thanks for all your support and encouragement. You took a chance when others wouldn't.

INTRODUCTION

As a professional chef who entertains quite often, I am constantly looking for ways to wow my guests with flavor. That flavor can come from spending 12 hours in the kitchen (laboring over a multicourse menu) or it can come from using creative ingredients, highlighted in a way my guests have never imagined. The latter technique is always my preference because it allows me to concentrate on impeccable seasonal ingredients simply prepared—my signature way of cooking. And most importantly, it lets me be a guest at my own table.

In my mother's kitchen, I learned that Italian cuisine is essentially a cuisine of preservation: Fresh meats became pancetta and prosciutto; milk turned into cheese; grapes became wine and wine became vinegar; olives were brined or cured for eating, or pressed for oil. In the case of oils and vinegars, we took it a step further and also used them to preserve foods as diverse as wild mushrooms we collected from the surrounding woods and our own garden-fresh tomatoes. The quality of our family meals depended entirely on the quality of our harvest.

In today's world, it's not necessary to preserve our summer bounty in order to sustain life through a lean winter. But it's still challenging to find ingredients that will bring convenience to our cooking without compromising quality or creativity. With this book, you will learn as I have that cooking with homemade flavored vinegars and oils adds a little culinary magic to every meal.

A Word About Oils

Whenever my *nonna* (grandmother) made tomato sauce from her own canned tomatoes, she would send my mother to the basement for a spoonful of *conserva*, a mixture of pureed dried tomatoes and olive oil. The intensity of flavor added a mouthful of summer to her wintertime sauce. She also used the flavorful oil that floated to the top of the *conserva* to drizzle over vegetables roasted atop her wood-fired stove.

This aromatic *conserva* was my first exposure to infused oils. It was a product, a by-product really, of a way of life. At the end of summer my family began preserving the harvest to eat through the winter. We dried the tomatoes on big sheets outdoors. When they were three-quarters dried, they were pureed with olive oil, put in a large crock, and carried to the basement. The lid was another layer of olive oil. As the *conserva* sat, the oil would naturally separate out and float to the top. The oil's passage through the sun-ripened and dried tomatoes gave the *conserva* all the flavor of the summer garden.

Making infused oils harnesses the flavor of an ingredient and often makes it easier to use that flavor in cooking. For instance, I love the taste of lavender and use a lavender-infused oil in several dishes, including a roast salmon (page 86). Or I use a simple marinade made with basil oil (page 29) to reinvent a classic roasted chicken. A pasta dish like Mushroom and Artichoke Pappardelle (page 82) draws new inspiration using porcini oil, which gives this one-dish meal a terrific, earthy flavor.

Flavored oils capture and preserve the aroma and flavor of an herb at the peak of its season, add depth and strength to kitchen pantries, and shorten cooking times. They work in the kitchen as a condiment—try a drizzle on top of foods such as pasta, bruschettas, vegetables, and fish and to stir into sauces and soups. They also work as an ingredient—you can substitute for the fresh ingredient when it has gone out of season, or if you have not had time to go to the store. In addition, because these flavored oils are made with olive oil, they are versatile and easy to use—as much at home for sautéing as for making vinaigrettes and sauces.

I have included several techniques for making flavored oils at home. One is used for soft-leaved green herbs such as basil, chervil, and mint; another for more resinous herbs such as lavender, rosemary, and oregano, plus separate methods for roasted garlic and citrus flavored oils.

There are an increasing number of good flavored oils on the market. Flavored oils will vary in flavor depending on the production process, as well as the quality and the specific blend of their ingredients. Taste them before you use them! Flavored oils are so incredibly versatile, you might soon find yourself using them in nearly every dish you cook. Hopefully, these recipes will encourage you to experiment and explore further.

A Word About Flavored Vinegars

Cooking is more fun and more soul satisfying when the cook has some involvement with the ingredients for a dish. Participation can be as basic as making your own vinegar or simply shopping carefully to find the best and most interesting vinegar to enhance your cooking style. By thinking ahead—taking advantage of seasonal ingredients or remembering to stop at a certain specialty shop—the work can be spread out to fit even the most compressed schedule.

Making homemade vinegar speaks to me because it is part of my family heritage. My mother made vinegar from wine that my father made. She made vinegar from all sorts of fruits as well, first fermenting their juice and then making vinegar.

As a young chef, heading up the Tra Vigne Restaurant kitchen in the Napa Valley, I went beyond making a few wine vinegars. I used vinegar as a way to preserve the flavors of fruits, herbs, and vegetables. Traditionally French raspberry vinegar was made by dropping a few berries into a bottle and filling it with vinegar. That would yield a pretty look, but it never delivered on the flavor front. I wondered what would happen if we took a wonderful purée of perfectly ripe berries, added some vanilla, then just enough vinegar to sharpen the berries and keep them from fermenting. Well, the results surpassed even my wildest expectations: We were we all dazzled by the amazing flavor! I immediately began using them as fat-free dressings, deglazes for various sautéed meats and fish, or as simple last-minute marinades before we grilled meats and vegetables. This use of flavored vinegar quite radically changed my cooking.

When you are excited by the colors, aromas, tastes, and textures of your ingredients—and their potential to expand your repertoire of delicious, easily prepared dishes—you will want to cook! These recipes will show you how easy it is to make a wine vinegar that will far surpass most of the commercial vinegars on the market. You will also be able to make herbal, fruit, and savory vinegars in just a few minutes. And you will discover that vinegar is one of the kitchen's great "fat-free flavor savers."

When it is time to cook with your vinegar, the ideas and techniques may be as simple as brushing fruit vinegar on fish or poultry before grilling or broiling. More time-consuming recipes are easily done ahead and even frozen. And when you do serve them, they will taste so astoundingly good, your guests or family will ask for them again and again.

The recipes in this book are broken up in two sections, Flavored Oils and Flavored Vinegars, then grouped into chapters based on flavor (such as oils infused with basil, chiles, or citrus or vinegars flavored with rosemary, wine, or raspberries). Each chapter presents simple, easy-to-prepare recipes using these oils and vinegars, including salads, pasta, fish, meat, and vegetable dishes, plus a few basic sauces and marinades. There is no need for fancy equipment—a big pot for cooking pasta and blanching vegetables, a deep sauté pan, and a few baking dishes and you're ready to go. Many of the recipes are modern adaptations of family recipes I learned from my mother, dishes we enjoyed in our home every day. My hope is that your success with each dish will inspire you to cook more, and more often, and to spread the pleasure of good eating to all your family and friends.

A Bit of Final Advice

Before you start cooking, I would like to give you a few very simple, basic rules. They may contradict some of what you have been taught but, if you follow them, I guarantee you will become a better cook!

◦ Don't cook if you don't want to.
◦ Don't cook when you are full.
◦ Shop when you are hungry.
◦ Cook with those ingredients in the biggest displays. This is usually
the produce at the peak of its season.
◦ Make the food your own—substitute and experiment—never say
"I can't make it" just because you don't have that exact ingredient.

Part 1

FLAVORED OILS

No ingredient plays a more important role in an Italian kitchen than olive oil. When I arrived in the Napa Valley in 1986 to take over the kitchen at Tra Vigne, I needed to find an olive oil to match my style of cooking. My traditional Italian upbringing (in central California but still very Old World) made me want to make one of my own. It had to be a dual-purpose oil, good for cooking and as a condiment.

I began working with various producers of California olive oil and in 1988 bottled our first extra-virgin oil for our Olio Santo label. It was and is still a blend of Mission and Manzanillo olives. The oil tastes fruity, full bodied, and rich and takes the heat well, maintaining its flavor. With this introduction to California olive oil, I became curious about the old olive groves I noticed scattered throughout the Napa Valley and wondered how an olive oil made from the fruit of those trees would taste.

I discovered some of the groves, lost in tangles of brush, oaks, and manzanita, while mushroom hunting in the hills surrounding Napa Valley. They did not look like any olive varieties I had seen before. Learning what sort of oil those trees could produce would mean harvesting and pressing the olives in separate small batches, grove by grove. At that time, I could find no one with the capacity to process such small amounts of olives. On a trip to Italy, I found a small, one-half-ton mill and press and brought it back to the Napa Valley. In 1991 I began pressing olives from these old groves and those of neighbors.

These old trees stand witness that California has a long olive-growing history. Olives arrived in California after 1769 with the Spanish-born Franciscan missionaries. They planted the land surrounding their missions with essentials of their religious practice and diet: most notably grapes, olives, and wheat. The already established missions in Baja California probably supplied the planting stock for the new California missions, which spread from San Diego to Sonoma, just west of the Napa Valley.

To plant olives, one must have a long-term commitment: The olive trees the padres tended would not bear fully until they were about five years old and would not be considered mature until they were thirty. They would outlive the original Franciscans by decades and continue to produce until they were well over a century in age. Mission olives, brought by the Franciscans and named after the missions where they were first introduced in California, are still the most widely planted variety.

In the 1870s and 1880s California's olive oil industry profited from the importation of many other European olive varieties. New groves were established and press houses sprung up all over the state, including small ones in Napa Valley. Many of the press houses were owned by large olive grove proprietors who sold cured olives in bulk as well. There was not yet an olive canning industry.

Since then, the state's olive oil business has ridden a boom-and-bust roller coaster. Good olive oil is expensive because of the hand labor required by production, the slowness of the trees to produce, and their inconsistent crop bearing. These qualities help make cultivating olives for olive oil production a business vulnerable to competition.

The invention of the canned ripe olive at the turn of the century sounded the death knell of California's olive oil industry. Canned olives are more profitable than olive oil. In addition, before World War I, cheap, imported olive oil flooded the market. These oils were adulterated with cheaper oils of other types. Eventually, such adulterations of oils and other food products would lead to the Pure Food and Drug Act. California producers fought the imports by telling customers to buy California oil to ensure they were purchasing pure, unadulterated olive oil. This is perhaps the origin of the now outdated label terminology: pure olive oil.

Our producers enjoyed a respite from cheap competition during the First World War when most of the olive oil–producing countries of Europe were at war. At the close of the war, cheap imports again became available until World War II, when the pattern repeated itself. During this upheaval many groves were abandoned and forgotten as underbrush grew up around the old trees. Other groves were grafted to canning varieties, which have small pits and more flesh than olives for olive oil.

In the last fifteen years we have experienced an abrupt change. Quite suddenly, there is a resurgent interest in olive oil and its potential quality in California. My own experiments reflect a broader trend. The attitude and excitement is reminiscent of our wine industry when we began to understand we could produce wines equal to the best in the world. As it is, California now grows 99 percent of all olives produced in the United States.

The motivating factor, as it was in the wine industry, has been an educated, demanding consumer. In an enthusiastic heat to get started, the new and hopeful olive oil producers have done everything at once: hired consultants, unearthed and imported traditional equipment including milling stones, set up press houses, harvested from trees thought only decorative a few years ago, imported olive varieties from France and Italy to plant, and bottled single-estate olive oils.

Because of the high cost of land, equipment, and labor, California will most likely remain a very small producer of olive oil by world standards. My hope is that we will continue to experiment and refine our techniques in order to create oils that are truly expressive of the land and the people, and thus ideally suited to the local cuisine.

CALIFORNIA OLIVE OIL PRODUCTION

In many parts of the world, it is not unusual for a property (anything from a small farm to a large estate) to produce much of the food eaten at its table. Wine, bread, fruit, vegetables, olive oil, meat—all could be grown, harvested, and processed on the same land. Because the soil, the climate, and the people are different on each property, the products it produces develop unique flavors. My dream is to incorporate some of this philosophy into the lifestyle of the inhabitants of Napa Valley.

Olives and olive oil are never the same year to year. Weather conditions vary and the quality and crop level of the olive tree will display these variations. Olive trees of the same type—and there are hundreds of varieties grown for olive oil production—growing a short distance apart in the Napa Valley will produce olive oils that reflect in their taste the very specific conditions surrounding them: the amount of sunlight and water as well as the amount and type of nutrients in the soil. Each variety of olive adds to nuance of character, as do the grower's decisions that affect each tree, most importantly pruning technique and the timing of harvest.

The old groves I work with now to produce individual bottlings had not been pruned in many years. These trees have grown tall; olives are usually pruned into a short, spreading shape to ease hand harvesting and to encourage crop yield. Olive trees bear only on that year's growth, so the crop an unpruned tree bears is sparse and the olives are small. Restoring a grove to production takes time and involves some risk. Over time, as the trees are properly cared for, the crop will change to produce more and fatter olives, hopefully. Only after ten years or so of cultivation and production will I know whether their oil has been worth the effort. For instance, some groves were planted as rootstock, not as fruit-bearing trees. These may never produce good olive oil, and they are too old to graft.

Olives picked early in the season, while they are still green, tend to produce oils with a deep green color and peppery flavors particularly well suited for beans, vegetables, game, and meat. Those picked later in the season, when the olives have begun to change color—from green to a reddish purple—often have a straw-like color and soft, fruity flavors with a vanilla quality good for use with fish.

Production processes are relatively simple and require lots of hard work. Pickers of early-harvest olives tape their fingers and strap a basket to their chests. They rake the olives with their fingers off the limbs into the baskets. It is very hard work—green olives cling hard to the tree.

Later in the season, the olives hang more loosely from the tree. In Europe, nets are spread on the ground or suspended under each tree and the limbs are beaten and raked with long poles. There are also mechanical harvesters that grab each tree by the trunk and shake it vigorously. In California, almost all olives are picked green and therefore must be harvested by hand. Now, growers are experimenting with various planting and training systems to allow mechanical harvesting. A full 60 percent of the cost of producing olive oil pays for picking labor alone. Cost-effective harvesting is the biggest stumbling block to building a larger olive oil industry.

Olives must not be bruised or otherwise damaged during picking or processing. Just as a bruise on a peach or pear can lead to rot within a short time, in olives, damage begins a process of oxidation that raises the acidity level. The riper, black olives naturally have higher acidity than green and also are more easily bruised. Picking late-harvest olives in order to make virgin olive oil (which must have a low natural acidity) becomes a high-wire act.

After picking, the olives are crushed to a paste. The paste is then mixed, which allows the tiny droplets of oil within the cell structure of the olive to adhere to each other and form drops which may then be separated from the olive pits and residue. There are several methods of crushing and mixing, the most picturesque and traditional of which is the massive, stone mill. Two huge, rotating stones crush the olives very slowly between them. The movement of the stones and their slowness allows mixing to take place at the same time. Olives may also be crushed by a hammer mill. Its many small heads shaped like hammers quickly crush the olives by beating them into a paste. The paste must then be mixed well to allow the small droplets of oil to adhere to each other; when well mixed, the paste has a shiny, oily look.

Now the liquid contents of the olives (oil and water) must be separated from the solids, and then the water separated from the oil. In the traditional method, the olive paste is spread on round mats that are stacked in a mechanical hydraulic press. As pressure is applied, the oil and water begin to flow. The oil must then be separated from the water, usually by centrifuge.

The finest oils come from the first light pressing accomplished mostly by the weight of the stacked mats themselves. As the pressure increases so does acidity, and quality decreases. These lesser oils are then refined—corrected for color, flavor, and acidity—before sale. The oil in the remains of the paste is extracted with the aid of solvents, then refined, resulting in an odorless, flavorless oil that is then blended with better oils for taste and sold as olive pomace oil.

Not all olive oils are pressed. To qualify as a virgin or extra-virgin olive oil, the oil must be produced by only mechanical or physical methods (no chemicals are allowed) and have a natural acidity below a specified level. Two other mechanical means are selective filtration (invented in 1911 in Spain) and centrifugation. Selective filtration works on the principal of oil's natural attraction to metal. Stainless steel plates are dipped into the paste, and the oil adheres to them; they are then lifted and drip oil into a receiving vessel.

In centrifugation, a heavy-duty decanting centrifuge swirls the paste, throwing oil and water in one direction and the solids in another. A second centrifuge immediately separates oil and water. Quickly separating the new oil from the water is very important as the oil can pick up off flavors if left too long in contact with the vegetative water.

Olive oil easily picks up flavors and aromas—an inconvenience and quality deterrent when too many leaves and stems are left with the olives when crushed or if the oil is not separated from its water fast enough. This vulnerability becomes an advantage when your interest is in making flavored (infused) oils.

One of the first uses of olive oil was as a flavored oil: Romans added aromatic substances to olive oil, which was almost always rancid because of the primitive extraction techniques, and used it cosmetically, rubbing it on their bodies as a moisturizer. Making what we know now as high-quality olive oil was not possible until early in the last century when rectification processes were developed. Once the olive oil is made, it is analyzed for acidity. Extra-virgin and virgin olive oils receive no further processing; oils with higher acidity levels are refined—corrected for color, aroma, and flavor to produce a clean, neutral-tasting oil. A percentage of virgin or extra-virgin olive oil is added to this neutral oil to give it flavor and it is sold simply as olive oil.

Just before bottling, most olive oils are filtered to remove tiny olive particles and produce a brilliant, clear color. Some people prefer unfiltered olive oils, although it is very difficult to distinguish any difference in taste.

Olive oil grades are determined by acidity levels. Taste varies according to the house style of the producer. Virgin and extra-virgin oils will show variations according to vintage as well. Olive oil is actually a fruit juice, the juice of olives, and is therefore perishable. Look for bottling or harvest dates and buy oil as fresh as possible. Store it in a cool, dark place. Once opened, use within a relatively short time.

EXTRA-VIRGIN OLIVE OIL AND VIRGIN OLIVE OIL

All virgin olive oil is extracted from olives only by mechanical means. The resulting oil must experience no treatments other than washing, decantation, centrifugation, and filtration. The oil's flavor must be without flaw. Two levels of virgin oil are sold in the United States: extra-virgin olive oil and virgin olive oil. The primary difference is their acidity level.

EXTRA-VIRGIN OLIVE OIL is the highest virgin oil quality grade. These oils have a distinctive taste ranging from soft and fruity to peppery depending on methods and timing of harvesting and handling as well as olive variety and specific growing conditions. The acidity is less than 1 percent.

VIRGIN OLIVE OIL also has individual taste characteristics though it is not as fine as extra-virgin olive oil. Its acidity varies from 1 to 3 percent.

OLIVE OIL (once called pure olive oil) is the name for a blend of refined olive oil and virgin olive oil. Some virgin oil is not considered edible without refining, usually because its acidity is too high or it has taste flaws. Refining results in a clean, neutral-tasting oil. Typically, 5 to 10 percent or more virgin or extra-virgin olive oil is blended with the refined oil for flavor and balance.

OLIVE POMACE OIL is not a quality grade of olive oil. It is oil extracted with the use of solvents from the remains of the olive paste after extraction of olive oil by other means. This oil is then refined to produce a neutral oil and blended with virgin olive oil for flavor and body.

LIGHT OLIVE OIL is not a quality grade of olive oil nor does it have anything to do with calories. It is not healthier than any other olive oil. Instead, it is a marketing gimmick to describe the oil's flavor. Light olive oil is an olive oil blended for its light (neutral) taste. To me, it is nonsense to pay more for less. Try a light oil and a less expensive olive oil and see if you can tell the difference.

Whatever the quality grade or blend, all olive oils are created equal in calories and fat grams. Since olives are a fruit, they contain no cholesterol. The United States has defined a serving portion of olive oil as one tablespoon. One tablespoon contains 14 grams of fat and 120 calories, all of which are from fat. However, olive oil has proportionately very little harmful saturated fat, which raises blood cholesterol, and lots of the more beneficial monounsaturated and polyunsaturated fats. Olive oil is 77 percent monounsaturated fat, which has been shown to reduce low density lipoprotein (LDL—the kind of cholesterol you don't want) circulating in the blood while high density lipoprotein (HDL—the good cholesterol) levels remain unchanged.

I am often asked why I cook with extra-virgin olive oil for all types of cooking including sautéing. My questioners have been taught such use is a waste of expensive oil. My response is though some flavor is lost, the resulting dish will taste better than if a lower-quality oil were used. There are times, however, when extra-virgin oil is not appropriate.

For instance, I use simple olive oil when the strong olive taste of an extra-virgin oil would interfere with a preparation, such as in a mayonnaise. For the same reason, I use simple olive oil when making flavored oils. For me, the point of flavored oils is that the oil carries the herbal flavor throughout a dish in a way that adding fresh herbs may not. I want the herbal flavor to dominate and the olive oil to be a supporting flavor.

1 MAKING AND USING FLAVORED OILS

If you look closely at Italian cooking, you will discover it is a cuisine of preservation, born of a necessity to conserve ingredients in season for eating out of season—grapes into wine, pork into prosciutto and pancetta, milk into cheese, tomatoes into sauce and dried tomatoes, olives into olive oil. Flavored oils in Italian cooking were not an end in themselves, they were a by-product of something else: the tomato-scented oil covering dried tomatoes, the aromatic oil preserving a harvest of wild mushrooms.

Making flavored oils grew naturally out of my style of cooking. I think of my style as having three components—impeccable ingredients, solid technique, and a degree of fantasy. Flavored oils include all three aspects—intensely flavored herbs, the infusion technique, and color and versatility, which take them into the realm of fantasy. Whenever used, infused oils add these same dimensions to any dish. For

instance, fresh mozzarella with vine-ripened tomato and basil is transformed by basil oil's intense aromas and brilliant green color. And esoteric flavors such as lavender (which is usually only seen in culinary use as part of herbes de Provence or sugared as a cake decoration) extracts wonderfully into olive oil and can then be used as a cooking ingredient. I mix it with honey and balsamic vinegar as a marinade for roasted salmon (page 86).

There are also technical reasons to cook with flavored oils. The role of oil and other fats in cooking is at least two-fold: They add richness and carry flavor into a dish, increasing the amount of perceived flavor. Flavored oils make their intense flavors immediately available whether using mushroom, garlic, or rosemary. Fresh herbs cooked long enough in a dish to disperse their flavors will lose freshness. When added at the end of the cooking process, their effect often goes unnoticed. But flavored olive oils disperse their flavor throughout a dish immediately and maintain their fresh herbal flavor.

Flavored oils also can add depth and strength to your cooking with their versatility, flavor, and convenience. Use them, without plan, as a condiment: to drizzle on top of pasta, pizza, and bruschetta; to finish dishes by floating a spoonful in soups and sauces; or as a sauce substitute on meats and vegetables. As an ingredient, oils infused with fresh herbs substitute for the fresh herb. Dried herbs are not really an adequate substitute for fresh; their flavors are unto themselves. Recipes usually list dried herbs as a substitute for fresh (including recipes in this book) as a compromise only.

A few practical words of advice before you begin your explorations: Your flavored oils will only have as much flavor as the ingredients you use. I recommend using a simple olive oil so the herb or vegetable flavor of the infusion will dominate. Although amounts of flavoring ingredients are given, making flavored oils is not an exact science. Results depend on the freshness and flavor strength of the herbs, vegetables, and spices. Different varieties even of the same herb have varying intensities of flavor. Whether it is early, late, or the height of the season for the ingredients also affects flavor. Grow your own herbs, ask a friend, or go to farmers' markets and smell and taste the herbs before infusing them. If you use tired, old basil, for example, your flavored oil will also taste old and tired.

Make small batches of oil and refrigerate them to preserve their flavor. You will gain confidence faster with small batches—successful experiments can be repeated, unsuccessful ones forgotten. Use the oils within a week to take advantage of the freshness of their flavor. My style of cooking accentuates big, strong flavors. If you prefer more subtle flavors, cut down the amount of flavoring ingredients.

Following are several methods (with variations) for infusing flavors into olive oil. They are faster and result in stronger flavors than the traditional method of putting several sprigs of an herb in olive oil and waiting several weeks or a month before use. Use the cold method for delicate herbs such as basil, cilantro, and chervil, and a variation of that method for garlic.

The best method for making roasted garlic oil, in my opinion, is by roasting whole garlic heads in ample amounts of olive oil so you get both the rich-tasting paste and the flavored oil. Use the warm method for spices and for more resinous herbs including rosemary and oregano, and a variation of that method for chilies or mushrooms. I have developed another method for citrus. In Tuscany, occasionally whole lemons will be crushed with the whole olives into a paste and pressed so that the lemon becomes an integral part of the oil's flavor. It is a delicate process and the oils are very expensive. The results you will have with the method outlined here emphasize the fresh, juicy flavor of citrus. Orange works particularly well and I love it with beets and tomatoes. Just make sure the oranges are sweet, juicy, and have a just-picked aroma. I have had great luck with navel oranges.

Filtering the oils requires some degree of patience. This is especially true for the cold infusion method in which you purée the herb in the oil. For a filter, I have had the most luck with cheesecloth, which I rinse and squeeze dry first. But any cotton cloth will do—a sheet, clean rag, tea towel, napkin— as long as you rinse it well first to remove any smell or taste of detergent. For the warm infusion method, filter the oil while still warm; it goes much faster!

ROASTED GARLIC PASTE AND OIL

Makes about ¾ cup garlic paste and ⅓ cup roasted garlic oil; or ¾ cup roasted garlic oil if using 1 cup oil

1 pound whole garlic heads
(6 to 8 whole heads garlic)

½ cup extra-virgin olive oil
(use 1 cup for roasted garlic oil)

Salt and freshly ground pepper

Serve roasted garlic hot from the oven with grilled bread and a salad or make a paste to spread on pizza or to mix by the spoonful into soups, stews, and sauces for extra flavor. To make roasted garlic oil, simply double the amount of oil.

Preheat oven to 375 degrees F. Slice off top ⅓ of each garlic head and discard or save for another use. Peel off outer layers of skin. Place close together in a shallow baking dish just large enough to hold the garlic. Pour oil over garlic and season amply with salt and pepper. Cover with aluminum foil and bake until cloves begin to pop out of their skins, about 1 hour. Uncover and bake another 15 minutes or until golden brown.

To make the paste, squeeze the garlic cloves into a bowl and mash. To store, cover with a thin layer of the olive oil in which it baked and refrigerate up to 2 days. Reserve baking oil in a tightly covered, sterilized glass jar or bottle and use within 1 week.

Chef's Notes

The roasted garlic-flavored baking oil is wonderful simply added to vinaigrettes, for sautéing vegetables, or in any of the recipes calling for roasted garlic oil.

GARLIC FLAVORED OIL
Cold Infusion Method

Makes about ¾ cup

1 head raw garlic, separated into cloves and peeled
(about ⅓ cup finely chopped)

½ cup distilled white vinegar

1 cup olive oil

Choose unblemished garlic without cracks or soft spots. For roasted garlic oil, see recipe above.

Soak cloves in vinegar 15 minutes, drain, and rinse under cold, running water. Drain, dry well, then put in blender with oil and pulse until chopped. Do not blend to a purée or the oil and garlic will be too difficult to separate!

Strain purée immediately through a fine-mesh strainer such as a china cap. Strain again through 4 layers of cheesecloth and put in a sterilized glass bottle. Cover tightly and refrigerate. Use within 1 week for optimum flavor.

HERB FLAVORED OILS
Cold Infusion Method

2 cups tightly packed soft-leaved green herb
(such as basil, chervil, chives, cilantro, mint)

1 cup olive oil

Chef's Notes

Tarragon does not work very well except early in the spring when it is very sweet, otherwise it tends to taste bitter when infused. Make sure to squeeze all the water out of the cheesecloth or filter papers before use.

For the best results, choose very fresh herbs with strong flavors and an olive oil with a clean, neutral taste. A blender makes a finer, smoother purée than a food processor and extracts more flavor. Some oil will be lost during filtering depending on how tightly it binds to the flavoring ingredients.

Bring a large saucepan of water to a boil. Add herbs and make sure to push the leaves under the boiling water. Blanch herbs 5 seconds. Drain into a strainer and immediately plunge into a bowl of ice water. Drain well and squeeze out all liquid. Purée in a blender with olive oil.

Strain purée immediately through a fine-mesh strainer such as a china cap. Strain again through 4 layers of cheesecloth and put in a sterilized glass bottle. Cover tightly and refrigerate. Use within 1 week for optimum flavor.

CITRUS FLAVORED OIL

2 medium oranges
or 3 lemons, Meyer lemons, or limes, cut in eighths

1 cup olive oil

Chef's Notes

If lemons have thick skins, the pith may add some bitterness to the oil. To avoid this, peel the zest with a vegetable peeler, put in a food processor, and chop finely. Cut the pith off the fruit being careful not to cut into the pulp. You want to save as much juice and pulp as possible. Cut the fruit into eighths and process with the zest. Then put in a stand mixer and mix as above.

This method results in an oil that captures the fresh flavor of citrus. Look for fruit with thin skins—the more pith, the more bitter the flavor. If you can only find fruit with thick skins, see Chef's Notes. Orange is a knockout. Try tangerines and kumquats, too. You can also make an oil with both an orange and a lemon though I prefer the clear flavor of the single fruit.

Roughly chop the fruit—skin, seeds, and all—in a food processor with short pulses or use a chef's knife. Do not process to a purée. If the fruit is too finely chopped, the oil will emulsify with the pulp and not separate. Transfer the fruit to the work bowl of an electric mixer and add the oil. Mix on low speed 10 minutes with the paddle attachment. Let stand at room temperature 2 hours.

Rinse 4 layers of cheesecloth in cold water and squeeze dry. Suspend a fine-mesh strainer over a fat separator or bowl. Put the citrus mixture in the cheesecloth and squeeze to extract the oil. (As you squeeze, the web of cheesecloth loosens. The strainer will catch the bits of pulp which may escape.) Let stand again to allow oil and juice to separate. The clear oil will float above the thick mixture of juice, pulp, and some emulsified oil. Pour off oil into a sterilized glass jar or bottle and discard juice. Cover tightly, refrigerate, and use within 1 week.

VARIATION FOR KUMQUATS: Use ½ pound fruit for 1 cup oil and follow the method above. I have also seen limequats occasionally in the shops; they would make an intriguing oil. If you find them or grow them, be sure to try making a citrus oil with them.

1 ounce dried mushrooms, such as porcini or shiitake, or 4 fresh hot chilies (unseeded) or 8 dried chilies (of a single type or mix for more complex flavors)

1 cup olive oil

Chef's Notes

If you filter through coffee filters, rinse them and squeeze dry before use. You will need some patience and probably several filters. Pour the oil little by little and stir occasionally. You will recover almost all the oil if you use dried chilies; however, the more fresh chilies, the less chili oil since the oil will bind and be hard to separate after being infused.

DRIED MUSHROOM or CHILI OIL
Warm Infusion Method

Makes about ¾ cup mushroom oil; about 1 cup chili oil

Experiment with combinations of dried, fresh, and smoked chilies to add different flavor dimensions to your oil, not just heat. Try fresh poblanos, jalapeños, and serranos or dried anchos and pasillas. Roast one of the fresh or dried chilies to add flavor. Add black pepper to the mix. It makes a truly amazing oil! Mushroom oil can be made from packaged, dried mushrooms such as porcini and shiitake. Mushroom hunters can dry their less-than-perfect specimens and use them for oil.

Chop mushrooms or chilies in a food processor until fine. Place in a pot with the oil and heat until mixture begins to bubble. Remove from heat and let cool 10 to 15 seconds. Swirl until just warm. Strain into a bowl through 4 layers of cheesecloth. Squeeze well to extract as much oil as possible. Pour into a sterilized jar or bottle, seal tightly, refrigerate, and use within 1 week for best flavor.

½ cup finely chopped fresh rosemary, sage, oregano, or lavender or ¾ cup (about 2 ounces) ground cumin, cinnamon, nutmeg, ginger, star anise, saffron, black pepper, or curry powder or ¼ cup chopped fresh ginger

1 cup olive oil

HERB or SPICE FLAVORED OILS
Warm Infusion Method

Makes about 1 cup

Use this method for tough-leafed herbs such as rosemary and sage as well as dried spices, or for dried mushrooms and fresh or dried chilies (see recipe above). Use the amounts of flavoring ingredients as a guide, feeling free to add more or less depending on the quality of your ingredients and your taste preferences. Dried spices extract very well and make delicious oils. For the best flavor, grind your own spices from the whole spice or buy a fresh supply of ground spices. The amount given at left will make a strongly flavored oil; you can dilute with more olive oil if desired.

Put herbs or spices and oil in a heavy saucepan. Heat over high heat until mixture begins to sizzle gently. Remove pan from heat, let cool about 10 seconds, and swirl contents until sizzling stops. Pour through a fine strainer or coffee filters into a sterilized bottle or jar. Press down on herbs to release last bit of oil and flavor. Seal tightly, refrigerate, and use within 1 week for best flavor.

TIPS
on Using Flavored Olive Oils

Flavored oils can add incredible versatility to any cook's repertoire. Once made, they shorten preparation time—no more picking fresh herbs from their stems and then mincing. And they add their flavor to a dish more evenly and rapidly than adding finely chopped fresh herbs.

Practicality, however, is not the best reason to buy or make flavored oils. The best reason is their own intense flavor and the creative potential they represent. One sniff of rosemary oil and a cook may recall the pan of tiny roasted potatoes with rosemary at a shop in a small, Italian coastal town. The fresh, summer smell of basil oil calls for plunging into—with raw or cooked vegetables, or just a piece of bread.

Suddenly, a cook—with several flavored oils on hand—has many options available to transform even standard recipes. Instead of reaching for olive oil to sauté garlic, reach for roasted garlic oil and go directly to adding vegetables such as spinach or broccoli. With a pinch of red pepper flakes or a spoonful of pepper oil to finish, you have a delicious dish to serve alongside chicken or to use as a pasta sauce. Don't feel guilty that cooking can be so easy, just enjoy it!

The recipes in this book are organized by flavor. However, each recipe will produce delicious results with extra-virgin or virgin olive oil and fresh herbs. Most of the recipes may also be varied themselves by substituting a different flavored oil than the one called for. Or try combining two oils with compatible flavors—rosemary and orange, for example—in a single dish. Following are some hints for using flavored oils in your cooking.

∘ Flavored oils are a cholesterol-free butter substitute. Dip bread into them or drizzle on toasted or grilled bread and any kind of potatoes, rice, polenta, or pasta. Dip bread sticks in flavored oil or brush them with rosemary, roasted garlic, or pepper oil before baking. Brush flavored oils on focaccia before baking or use flavored oils to give fresh flavor to commercial, prebaked pizza shells such as Boboli and even to drizzle on frozen or take-out pizza! Toss croutons with flavored oils and use them in salads and soups.

∘ Mix dried bread crumbs with garlic and rosemary oils, and toast in the oven until golden. Add grated Parmesan and fontina cheeses and use for gratins.

∘ Drizzle tomatoes with flavored oil before oven-drying them.

∘ Vinaigrettes, dressings, and marinades can be varied enormously by using flavored oils. A simple salad of mixed greens shows off the virtuosity of flavored oils. Use a citrus oil alone (no vinegar) to dress a salad, especially if you are serving good wines with your meal. Dressings make delicious sauces for fish, meats, and vegetables. There are several throughout this book.

∘ Dress up simple, fresh cheeses such as mozzarella and goat cheese by marinating them in flavored oils. This can be as simple as pouring a spoonful of oil over the cheese just before serving or leaving the two together for a day before serving.

∘ Make Hollandaise sauce with warmed flavored oils instead of clarified butter.

∘ Give soup (homemade, frozen, or canned) a taste perk with a flavored oil. Add oils to various tomato sauces.

∘ Fry eggs and home fries in pepper oil and serve them with grilled or toasted bread brushed with roasted garlic oil.

∘ Roast whole heads of garlic in rosemary or pepper oil to give both the garlic and the resulting oil an intriguing new flavor.

∘ Only a few flavored oils will stand up to high heat or even to low heat of long duration. The delicate flavors, especially those of basil and cilantro, will evaporate as they would if you exposed the raw ingredients to the same treatment. Some, such as rosemary, porcini, roasted garlic, and pepper oils, are sturdier. Roasted garlic, for instance, is already cooked, rosemary's resinous character makes it more resistant to high heat, and cooking will not destroy the heat of chilies though it may affect nuances of flavor. The flavor of porcini oil seems to become deeper and sweeter with heat. If you do choose to expose flavored oils to high heat, do so quickly, then add other ingredients to butter the effect and add more flavored oil to finish the dish with a fresher flavor.

∘ Store homemade flavored oils in clean glass jars and bottles and use within a week. Unopened commercial flavored oils should be stored in a cool, dark place and refrigerated once opened. They should be used within a month.

2 BASIL OLIVE OIL

Basil olive oil was the first infused oil I made. I worked backwards from pesto, taking out the cheese and nuts to make an olive oil and herb slurry. We used these slurries in the restaurant to great advantage and still use them: We make a tarragon slurry because tarragon, except for early in the season when it is very sweet, does not infuse well. Herbs, even when blanched first to set their color, can look dark and unattractive. The oil of the slurry, however, turned a beautiful, jeweled green color, so we began filtering the herbs out of the oil.

Basil is probably the most popular flavor for an infused oil and with good reason—all the things loved best about summer are concentrated in its aroma. I love basil oil simply for dipping bread or raw vegetables and for drizzling over vine-ripened tomatoes. But do not subject basil oil to high heat; you will lose a good deal of its flavor. And now you can enjoy pesto year round without using all your freezer space. Basil oil is the secret with parsley masquerading as basil.

🌿 BASIL DRESSING

½ cup plus 1 teaspoon basil olive oil (page 22)

1 teaspoon finely chopped garlic

1 tablespoon finely diced roasted red pepper (page 184)

2 tablespoons fresh lemon juice (preferably from Meyer lemons)

1 teaspoon black olive paste or tapenade (see Chef's Notes)

Salt and freshly ground pepper

The additions of roasted red pepper and olive paste give this vinaigrette the substance to dress vegetable and pasta salads served slightly warm or at room temperature.

Heat the 1 teaspoon basil oil in a small sauté pan over medium heat. Add garlic and cook slowly until transparent, about 2 minutes. Add roasted peppers and stir. Add lemon juice and mix well. Add remaining basil oil and olive paste and mix well again. Add salt and pepper to taste and remove from heat and let rest 1 to 2 minutes before mixing with a salad or pasta.

Chef's Notes

Olive paste and tapenade may both be made at home from whole black olives or purchased. Olive paste is a rough purée of olives; tapenade is also a purée of olives but flavored with anchovy and other seasonings.

🌿 BALSAMIC BASIL VINAIGRETTE

Makes about 1 ¼ cups

¼ cup balsamic vinegar

1 teaspoon finely chopped garlic

2 teaspoons finely chopped shallots

1 cup basil olive oil (page 22)

Salt and freshly ground pepper

This is a delicious all-purpose vinaigrette. Use it for any green salad, for vegetable salads such as grilled or roasted eggplant, and for main-dish salads such as green lentils and chicken. The recipe may be doubled.

Whisk together vinegar, garlic, and shallots in a small bowl. Whisk in basil oil and season to taste with salt and pepper. Keeps up to 4 days refrigerated in a tightly sealed container.

Chef's Notes

Balsamic vinegar can vary greatly in quality and strength. This recipe was written for less expensive vinegar. If you use an aged balsamic, you might want to reduce the quantity.

BASIL MARINADE

Makes about 1 cup

This basic marinade gives poultry and fish an aromatic flavor without masking their own delicate flavors. It is also good for marinating vegetables before roasting or grilling.

Put all ingredients in a food processor or blender and process 20 seconds. Place poultry or fish in a nonreactive dish and pour marinade over it. Cover, refrigerate, and let marinate—depending on the size of what is being cooked—15 minutes for thin fillets, 3 hours for chicken pieces.

When ready to cook, remove from marinade and cook to desired doneness. Discard marinade.

½ cup basil olive oil (page 22)

1½ teaspoons finely chopped garlic

½ small yellow onion, roughly chopped

2 tablespoons chopped fresh tarragon or 2 teaspoons dried tarragon (rehydrated, see Chef's Notes)

¼ cup dry white wine

Chef's Notes

To release the flavor of the dried tarragon, rehydrate it by mixing it with the white wine and let stand a few minutes before adding to the marinade.

BASIL OIL PESTO

Makes about 1½ cups

Basil Oil Pesto has innumerable uses—as a sauce for pasta and pizza, as a sandwich spread, a sauce for grilled or roasted meats, poultry, and fish, and even as a flavorful addition to soups and stews.

Remove tough stems from parsley and discard. Blanch parsley very quickly in rapidly boiling, salted water to brighten and stabilize the color. Plunge immediately in a bowl of ice water to stop the cooking, then drain well and squeeze out excess water.

Spread parsley on a cutting board and roughly chop it. Place it in a blender and add remaining ingredients except Parmesan cheese, salt, and pepper; blend until smooth. Pulse in Parmesan. Season with salt and pepper to taste. Sauce keeps up to 2 days, refrigerated, in a tightly sealed container. May also be frozen.

2 large bunches fresh flat-leaf parsley

1 cup basil olive oil (page 22)

1 tablespoon finely chopped garlic or ½ tablespoon roasted garlic olive oil (page 21)

2 tablespoons lightly toasted pine nuts (see page 185)

5 tablespoons freshly grated Parmesan cheese

Salt and freshly ground pepper

THE PLT—PANCETTA, LETTUCE, AND TOMATO SANDWICH

I like to make this sandwich with a sandwich press. When I tested it at home, I used our waffle iron with the flat plates inserted. The bread is buttered on the outside and grilled with only the pancetta inside. When the bread is toasted, separate the sandwich, spread the basil mayonnaise on one side, add the remaining ingredients, then reassemble.

Cook pancetta in a skillet until crisp and drain on paper towels. Spread butter on one side of bread. Divide pancetta among 4 slices on the unbuttered side. Top with second slice, buttered side up. Put in a preheated sandwich press, a waffle iron fitted with flat plates, or a skillet placed over medium heat. If you use a skillet, press down firmly on the sandwich with a spatula. Cook until brown on one side, then turn and toast second side.

Separate sandwich halves and arrange tomato slices on top of pancetta. Spread each other half with 1 tablespoon basil mayonnaise. Add arugula and season with salt and pepper to taste. Close sandwiches and cut in half. Serve immediately.

6 ounces pancetta, cut into ¼-inch pieces

2 tablespoons unsalted butter, softened

8 slices rustic bread (such as crusty Italian bread), cut about ⅜ inch thick

2–3 vine-ripened tomatoes, sliced ¼ inch thick

4 tablespoons Basil-Garlic Mayonnaise (page 33)

About 3 cups loosely packed arugula

Salt and freshly ground pepper

Chef's Notes

For a more sophisticated flavor and presentation, use brioche baked in a square pain de mie pan or loaf shape. If the pancetta you buy is very fatty, you may want to buy a little more since it will lose so much volume when cooked.

PASTA with TOMATO VINAIGRETTE

8 medium vine-ripened red tomatoes, peeled, seeded, and finely chopped

2 tablespoons minced shallots

1 tablespoon minced garlic

6 tablespoons finely chopped fresh flat-leaf parsley

¼ cup fresh lemon juice (preferably from Meyer lemons)

1 cup basil olive oil (page 22)

Salt and freshly ground pepper

1½ pounds dried pasta (such as rigatoni or orecchiette)

1 cup freshly grated Parmesan or pecorino cheese

This is my favorite summer pasta. Every Sunday morning my daughters and I go into the garden and pick whatever is at its freshest and ripest and incorporate it into this tomato vinaigrette. We especially like sautéed zucchini, grilled eggplant, and roasted pepper. Paired with a chilled sauvignon blanc, the dish makes a complete summer supper, and the kitchen stays clean and cool. The idea of cooking in the summer is to free yourself to spend time with family and friends!

Mix together tomatoes, shallots, garlic, ¼ cup of the parsley, lemon juice, basil oil, and salt and pepper to taste in a nonaluminum bowl and let rest at room temperature 15 to 20 minutes to let flavors develop. If making farther ahead, do not salt until 15 minutes before serving, otherwise salt will draw all the water out of the tomatoes.

When ready to eat, bring a large pot of salted water to a boil and cook pasta until al dente. Drain well and toss with tomato vinaigrette. Add ½ cup cheese and mix well. Garnish each serving with additional cheese and parsley. Serve immediately.

Chef's Notes

This pasta is meant to be served slightly warm, just above room temperature. If you would like it warmer, place the bowl of tomato vinaigrette over the pasta pot while the pasta is cooking to let the steam warm it. The pasta shape is important: rigatoni and orecchiette (little ears or small shells) both hold the sauce. If you choose a smooth, straight shape such as spaghetti, the sauce will drain off into a pool at the bottom of the bowl. I also like capellini for this dish. It holds the sauce very well, but everyone must be ready to sit down and eat immediately when it is done!

GRILLED HALIBUT
WITH BASIL-ORANGE MARINADE

Serves 4

Reducing the orange juice intensifies its flavor and lessens the acidity. This allows marinating the fish without cold cooking it as in a ceviche. Serve the fish with a salad of thinly sliced fennel and red onions tossed with salt and pepper, basil oil, and unreduced orange juice.

Strain orange juice through a fine sieve into a nonaluminum saucepan. Add bay leaf and pepper-corns and bring to a boil. Simmer until reduced to ½ cup and let cool. Remove and discard bay leaf and peppercorns. Slowly whisk in basil oil to form an emulsion.

    Preheat grill or broiler. Put fish in a flat glass or enamel dish and pour ½ the marinade over the fish. Turn fish several times to coat evenly with marinade. Cover, refrigerate, and marinate at least 1 hour. Drain fish and discard used marinade. Season with salt and pepper. Grill until done, about 10 minutes per inch of thickness, depending on heat of the grill. When half cooked, turn and brush with some of the remaining marinade. Continue to grill until done. Serve immediately with remaining marinade as a sauce.

1½ cups fresh orange juice

1 bay leaf

8 whole black peppercorns

½ cup basil olive oil (page 22)

2 pounds halibut fillets,
cut into 4 equal pieces

Salt and freshly ground pepper

Chef's Notes

Be sure to liberally oil the grill or the fish will stick, or invest in a nonstick or cast iron insert for the barbecue. Depending on the thickness of the fish, it can be marinated for longer than an hour and up to 6 to 8 hours.

BASIL-GARLIC MAYONNAISE

Makes about ¼ cup

This is a basic mayonnaise which can be made with any flavored oil. If you want to make it without a flavored oil, use olive oil or a vegetable oil. Extra-virgin olive oil has too strong a flavor for mayon-naise. I like a little garlic in mayonnaise. If you don't, leave it out. Also, if you are concerned about using raw eggs, see variation at end of recipe.

Whisk garlic with egg yolk and vinegar in a bowl or process in a food processor or blender. Start whisking in the basil oil, drop by drop, to form an emulsion. If using a machine, add oil little by little with the machine running. As mixture forms an emulsion, add remaining oil in a slow, steady stream while whisking or processing continuously. Season to taste with salt and pepper and stir in chopped basil, if using. If a thinner consistency is desired, whisk in a little warm water, 1 teaspoon at a time.

VARIATION WITH PASTEURIZED LIQUID EGGS AND CHOLESTEROL-FREE LIQUID EGGS:
Follow directions on the package and use the equivalent of one whole egg for the mayonnaise recipes in this book. Cholesterol-free liquid eggs, such as Egg Beaters, are readily available and work for these recipes as well. Use ¼ cup liquid egg and 1 tablespoon vinegar or lemon juice and proceed with the recipe as written. The texture is very light but the emulsion does not break and it tastes very good. There is the added benefit of enjoy-ing mayonnaise without fear of cholesterol!

1 clove garlic, finely chopped

1 egg yolk

2 teaspoons champagne wine vinegar or freshly squeezed lemon juice

¾ cup basil olive oil (page 22)

Salt and freshly ground pepper

2 tablespoons finely chopped fresh basil (optional)

Chef's Notes

If sauce breaks (separates), start again with another yolk and add the broken sauce teaspoon by tea-spoon, whisking all the while (or processing) to form an emulsion. As emulsion forms, drizzle in remainder.

Pizza Dough (page 36)

½ cup Roasted Garlic Paste
(page 21)

½ cup Basil Oil Pesto
(page 29)

Coarse cornmeal,
for the baking sheet

4–5 large, vine-ripened tomatoes, of any color or variety,
sliced ⅛ inch thick

Salt and freshly ground pepper

1 cup freshly grated
Parmesan cheese

Chef's Notes

One of my pet peeves is pizza topping not spread close to the edge of
the dough. This means that all the
filling is eaten in the first and second
bites, leaving only crust for the last.
Not to mention a slice that will not
hold straight when picked up!

PESTO PIZZA WITH
ROASTED GARLIC AND TOMATO

Makes three 10-inch pizzas; or
serves 6 as supper with a salad

What could possibly be better on a hot summer day than a freshly made pizza redolent with the aromas of summer? Serve with a glass of sauvignon blanc or pinot bianco. The flavor of this pizza insists
on great tomatoes. Arrange the tomatoes to cover the entire pizza so the tomato flavor will be part
of every bite.

Preheat oven to 500 degrees F. Place baking sheet in oven to preheat.

Shape ⅓ of pizza dough into a 10-inch circle on a lightly floured board. Spread with
⅓ of the garlic paste. Be sure to spread to within a half inch of the edge (see Chef's Notes).
Sprinkle ⅓ of the pesto on dough and spread out smoothly on top of garlic paste.

Remove baking sheet from oven and sprinkle with cornmeal. Transfer pizza to baking
sheet and put in oven. Bake until light brown and bubbling, about 10 minutes. Remove pizza
from oven and quickly arrange sliced tomatoes on top. Do not overlap slices. Season with salt
and pepper to taste. Sprinkle with ⅓ of the Parmesan cheese and return pizza to oven another
2 to 3 minutes or until cheese melts. Immediately transfer to a board, cut, and serve. Repeat
for remaining two pizzas.

# PIZZA DOUGH

Makes about 2 pounds dough,
enough for three 10-inch pizzas

1 cake (0.6 ounce) fresh yeast
or 1 package active dry yeast

½ cup lukewarm water

3½ cups all-purpose flour plus
additional flour for kneading

½ cup whole wheat flour

1 cup water

2 tablespoons extra-virgin
olive oil plus additional oil
for brushing bowl and dough

2 teaspoons salt

Coarse cornmeal,
for baking sheet

Chef's Notes

If you freeze the pizza dough,
defrost and let rise in the
refrigerator. It triples and quadru-
ples in volume with this method so
be sure to use a large bowl and
watch carefully that it does
not overflow. You can roll out the
dough with a rolling pin but this
presses all the air out of the edges
and creates a very flat pizza.
Toppings that are slightly liquid,
such as tomato sauce, or that melt,
such as mozzarella, will leak
off and spill.

The recipe can be doubled if you would prefer a thicker crust than recommended here. To ensure a really crisp crust, bake the crust blond first (without any topping) until light brown. My mother would do this, baking the crust ahead of time. Then when I came in and was ready to eat, she would add tomato sauce and cheese and put it back in the oven. You might think flavored oils in the dough would give subtle variations; instead their flavor gets lost. Save the flavored oils to top the pizza.

Combine yeast, the warm water, and ½ cup of the flour in the bowl of an electric mixer. Let stand 15 minutes to activate yeast. Add the remaining 3 cups all-purpose flour, whole wheat flour, the 1 cup water, olive oil, and salt. Mix with the dough hook attachment on low, then increase speed to medium low until the dough comes away from the bottom of the bowl. Dough should be slightly moist. Knead another minute.

Turn dough out onto a lightly floured surface and knead gently until smooth, folding the dough over itself. Shape into a ball, flatten into a fat disc with the heel of your hand, and put in an oiled bowl. Cover with a damp towel and let rise in a warm place until doubled in bulk, about 1 hour. Punch down and cut into 3 equal pieces. Roll each into a ball. Dough may be frozen at this point (see Chef's Notes). Brush lightly with olive oil and let rise in a warm place, covered, in oiled bowls or on a floured board, until doubled in size, about 30 minutes.

When ready to bake, preheat oven to 500 degrees F. On a lightly floured surface, flatten ball into a disc and nudge the dough outward into a circle with your fingers (see Chef's Notes). Flour the dough and the board as needed. Pick up the dough and, holding it by the edge, feed the circle through your fingers. Let the dough hang from your fingers onto the board. It will stretch as you work around the edges.

Lay dough back down on board and nudge into shape. If it needs further stretching, drape it over the backs of your closed fists. (Try this even if you do not feel as dexterous as the man in the pizza parlor!) Pull your fists gently apart from each other so that you rotate and stretch the dough. Return the dough to floured board and nudge into place. It should be about ⅛ inch thick and about 10 inches in diameter. If dough tears, simply press torn edges together firmly. The irregularities of hand-shaping are part of the charm.

Put baking sheet in the oven to preheat. When hot, remove, sprinkle with coarse cornmeal, and transfer dough onto it. Top as specified in recipe. Bake in the hot oven about 10 minutes or until crust is brown and crisp. Repeat with remaining dough.

TIELLA—
SUMMER VEGETABLE GRATIN

Serves 6

Tiella is the Italian name for a low, shallow baking dish. In my family, we would say, "Please pass the tiella" when at the table. The name eventually came to mean this particular dish baked in the tiella pan. You may also wish to serve this gratin spread on small toasts as an appetizer, or use it to stuff ravioli.

In a large sauté pan, heat 2 tablespoons of the extra-virgin olive oil over medium-high heat until it almost smokes. Add yellow and green zucchini and quickly sauté over high heat until zucchini just begins to color, about 5 minutes. Add salt, pepper, and a pinch of thyme. Pour onto a baking sheet to cool.

Repeat cooking process with peppers, green beans, mushrooms, and onion, wiping out pan and adding 2 tablespoons fresh extra-virgin olive oil for each vegetable. Mushrooms and onion will take longer to brown because of their water and sugar content.

Heat remaining 2 tablespoons extra-virgin olive oil in a saucepan over medium-high heat. Add garlic and sauté quickly until light brown, about 1 minute. With a slotted spoon, take out half the garlic and put on top of the vegetables. Add the tomatoes to the saucepan and simmer until mixture thickens, 7 to 8 minutes. Add basil oil and then add salt and pepper to taste. Spread tomato mixture on a baking sheet to cool.

If planning to add the bread crumb topping, preheat oven to 450 degrees F. When all vegetables and tomatoes have cooled, gently toss together in a bowl and fold in ¼ cup of the Parmesan. Adjust seasoning as needed. At this point, the vegetables may be eaten as is or transferred to a baking dish for topping. Mix the bread crumbs with the remaining ¼ cup Parmesan and sprinkle evenly over the top. Bake until lightly browned, about 15 minutes. Serve warm.

¾ cup extra-virgin olive oil

1 yellow zucchini or yellow crookneck squash (about ½ pound), sliced into rounds ¼ inch thick

1 green zucchini (about ½ pound), sliced into rounds ¼ inch thick

Salt and freshly ground pepper

2 tablespoons chopped fresh thyme or 2 teaspoons dried thyme

1 large red bell pepper, seeded and cut into ¼-inch dice

½ pound green beans, cut diagonally into ¼-inch pieces

6 ounces fresh wild or domestic mushrooms, sliced ¼ inch thick

1 large yellow onion, chopped

2 tablespoons finely chopped garlic

2 cups vine-ripened tomatoes, peeled, seeded, and chopped, or good quality, canned plum (Roma) tomatoes

⅓ cup basil olive oil (page 22)

½ cup freshly grated Parmesan cheese

1 cup dried bread crumbs (optional)

3 OREGANO OLIVE OIL

Oregano enhances so many different foods that it is one of the most important herbs in an Italian kitchen. Americans use the dried version frequently, especially in pizza parlors, but use fresh oregano much less frequently. In a pot or the garden, it grows easily and abundantly. Clip the fast-growing tips that appear to have bolted for making flavored olive oil. These have the most intense flavor.

Despite their differences in flavor, oregano oil and basil oil are nearly interchangeable because of their uses in cooking.

They are often combined though I prefer to use one or the other. Try using oregano oil with citrus oil for summer cooking.

Oregano (and cilantro and even rosemary) can have a soapy quality to its flavor which does not appear when oregano is properly infused into oil. You can then intensify the herbal flavor of oregano without any side effects! Tomatoes and oregano taste especially good together. I have included an all-purpose tomato sauce and given variations in ingredients so it can be made summer and winter.

WHITE BEANS

1 cup dried cannelloni beans
(see Glossary)

2 cups chicken stock (page 42)
or canned, low-salt
chicken broth

½ small onion

½ carrot

1 stalk celery

1 bay leaf

Several prosciutto scraps
(optional)

Salt and freshly ground pepper

ROASTED PEPPER SAUCE
AND PASTA

2 tablespoons extra-virgin
olive oil

8 cloves garlic, thinly sliced

1 cup finely chopped
yellow onion

2 teaspoons red pepper flakes

6 tablespoons oregano olive oil
(page 24)

3½ tablespoons finely chopped
fresh flat-leaf parsley

1 pound dried rigatoni pasta

2 red bell peppers, roasted,
peeled, seeded, and julienned
(page 184)

1½ cups freshly grated Parmesan or pecorino cheese

Salt and freshly ground pepper

# RIGATONI with WHITE BEANS AND ROASTED PEPPERS

The combination of beans and pasta makes this dish true comfort food. In winter, serve it warm sprinkled generously with freshly grated Parmesan and drizzled with oregano olive oil. In summer, serve it cool piled on top of ripe tomato slices.

Put cannelloni beans in a large saucepan with 4 cups cold water and bring to a boil over high heat. Cover and let stand until tepid, about 1 hour. Drain and rinse beans and return them to the pan with 2 cups water, chicken stock, onion, carrot, celery, bay leaf, and prosciutto. Bring to a boil over high heat; then lower heat and simmer very slowly until beans are tender, 1 to 1½ hours depending on the size and age of the beans. Season with salt and pepper to taste 15 minutes before beans are done. Reserve beans and their cooking liquid. Discard vegetables.

Heat extra-virgin olive oil in a large saucepan over medium heat until hot. Add garlic, onion, and red pepper flakes and sauté over medium-low heat until onions are soft and translucent, 3 to 5 minutes. Add beans and their cooking liquid and simmer a few minutes to blend flavors. Add 4 tablespoons of the oregano oil and 2 tablespoons of the parsley. Mix well.

Meanwhile, bring a large pot of salted water to a boil and add pasta. Cook until al dente, drain, and rinse. (Can be cooked ahead of time; see Chef's Notes.)

Add cooked pasta to beans in saucepan with roasted red and yellow peppers and heat through. Stir in 1 cup of the cheese and season to taste with salt and pepper. Pour onto a heated platter or into a heated serving bowl and sprinkle with remaining ½ cup cheese and 1½ tablespoons parsley. Drizzle last 2 tablespoons oregano olive oil over all.

Chef's Notes

If you cook the pasta ahead of time, toss it with 1 to 2 tablespoons oil so it will not get gummy and stick together. Submerge in boiling water 10 seconds to reheat before adding to dish.

 # CHICKEN STOCK

5 pounds chicken bones
(fresh, if possible, not frozen)

½ pound roughly
chopped onions

¼ pound roughly
chopped carrots

¼ pound roughly chopped
celery (do not include leaves,
which give a bitter flavor)

2 bay leaves

6 whole black peppercorns

6 whole juniper berries
(optional)

6 sprigs fresh flat-leaf parsley
(optional)

6 sprigs fresh thyme (optional)

Chef's Notes
May be doubled and frozen.

I use blond chicken stock in the summer when my cooking is lighter in flavor to allow the fresh taste of bright summer vegetables to shine through. I like the richer, more caramelized flavors of brown chicken stock for fall and winter cooking.

Rinse bones with cold water, put in a stockpot or large saucepan, and cover with cold water. Let rest 10 minutes, then drain and rinse again. (This washes off the blood and allows a clearer stock.) Return chicken bones to the stockpot and cover with cold water by an inch. Bring to a boil, reduce heat, and simmer 30 minutes. Skim foam from surface frequently. Continue to skim until mixture stops foaming.

Add onions, carrots, celery, bay leaves, peppercorns, and juniper berries, if using. Simmer very slowly another 4 hours. If using parsley and thyme, add only for last 30 minutes of cooking. Strain stock into a bowl; discard bones and vegetables. Cover and refrigerate stock until fat rises to surface and hardens. Discard fat and refrigerate or freeze. Stock keeps, refrigerated in a tightly sealed container, about 3 days.

VARIATION FOR BROWN CHICKEN STOCK: Preheat oven to 450 degrees F. After rinsing and soaking bones put them in a roasting pan, put in oven, and roast until brown all over. Stir bones occasionally. When browned, put bones in a stockpot and follow method above. While stock is simmering, put vegetables in the roasting pan and brown in the oven. When brown, transfer vegetables to stockpot. Immediately put roasting pan over medium heat and add about ½ cup red wine or water. Deglaze pan, scraping up all the brown bits which cling to the sides and bottom of the pan. Add to the stock and continue as above.

SPIEDINI of PRAWNS with PANCETTA AND OREGANO DRESSING

Serves 6 as an entrée
(about 6 prawns per person)

The garlic and oregano dressing is served warm, so make it just before serving. Grilling the prawns over wood adds a wonderful flavor but they can also be broiled or even sautéed in a few tablespoons of oil. Serve the prawns with a cucumber, red onion, and yogurt salad.

Preheat grill or broiler. Wrap each prawn in a slice of pancetta. Thread wrapped prawns on skewers, about 5 or 6 per serving, and set aside until ready to cook.

Heat extra-virgin olive oil in a heavy saucepan until almost smoking. Add garlic cloves and roast until golden brown, 3 to 5 minutes. Watch them carefully so they do not burn. Remove smaller cloves as they brown or they will overcook. Let garlic cloves cool in their cooking oil. Strain, reserving oil and cloves separately. (Taste the oil. If it is not scorched-tasting, save it to add to marinades, vinaigrettes, etc.) Drain cloves on paper towels; then slice thinly.

To make the vinaigrette, slice scallions on the diagonal as thinly as possible using all the white parts and a little of the green. Put scallions and sliced garlic in a bowl with red pepper, parsley, vinegar, and oregano oil. Season to taste with salt and pepper.

Grill prawns until the pancetta is golden and prawns are cooked through, about 5 minutes depending on the heat of the grill. Turn once during cooking. To serve, spoon vinaigrette over prawns. Serve hot.

2 pounds large prawns with shells (size 16/20 or larger, see Chef's Notes), peeled and deveined

36 (about) very thin slices pancetta

6 bamboo skewers, soaked, or metal skewers

2 tablespoons extra-virgin olive oil

1 large head garlic, separated into cloves and peeled

3 scallions

1 small red bell pepper, seeded, and cut into ¼-inch dice

2 tablespoons finely chopped fresh flat-leaf parsley

2 tablespoons vinegar

¼ cup oregano olive oil (page 24)

Salt and freshly ground pepper

Chef's Notes

Prawns are sized by the average number found in 1 pound. Therefore, 16/20s means there are between 16 and 20 prawns per pound.

PAPPA AL POMODORO—TOMATO AND BREAD SOUP WITH OREGANO CROUTONS

This version of the classic Tuscan tomato and bread soup has more texture than the traditional recipe. I made it one summer when I thought my family and I could eat the production of six tomato plants. It is a soup to be made in the height of tomato season and no other time: July, August, and early September, not June and not October!

Preheat grill or broiler. Use your hands to lightly oil the tomatoes with 1 tablespoon of the extra-virgin olive oil and season with salt and pepper. Place on grill or under broiler until softened and skins have darkened and blistered. Do not cook tomatoes all the way through. Let tomatoes cool; then peel, seed, and chop. Put the tomatoes in a strainer over a bowl to catch the juice. Reserve separately; you should have about 3 cups pulp and 1 cup juice.

Heat remaining 2 tablespoons extra-virgin olive oil in a large saucepan over medium-high heat until hot. Add garlic and sauté until light brown, moving pan on and off heat as necessary to regulate temperature. Add reserved tomato juice and tomato paste and simmer until thick (tiny bubbles cover the surface). Add tomatoes and continue to simmer until thick but not dry. Season with salt and pepper to taste (it needs a lot of pepper) and add oregano oil. Let cool to room temperature.

Preheat oven to 400 degrees F. Mix together in a bowl bread cubes, oregano oil, Parmesan, and salt and pepper to taste. Spread on a cookie sheet or in an oven-going skillet and bake until light brown, about 15 minutes. Immediately remove from oven. Be careful as croutons will continue to darken once removed from oven.

Toss arugula in a bowl with lemon juice, oregano oil, and salt and pepper to taste. Add half the croutons and toss again. Put a large spoonful of soup in each of 4 soup plates and garnish with arugula, remaining croutons, and Parmesan.

SOUP

3 pounds vine-ripened red tomatoes

3 tablespoons extra-virgin olive oil

Salt and freshly ground pepper

2 tablespoons finely chopped garlic

1 tablespoon tomato paste

¼ cup oregano olive oil (page 24)

OREGANO CROUTONS

2 cups ½-inch bread cubes cut from crusty Italian bread

2 teaspoons oregano olive oil (page 24)

2 tablespoons freshly grated Parmesan cheese

Salt and freshly ground pepper

GARNISH

2 bunches arugula

2 teaspoons freshly squeezed lemon juice

3 tablespoons oregano olive oil (page 24)

Salt and freshly ground pepper

Parmesan cheese

Chef's Notes

Grilling the tomatoes brings up their flavor in the same way as adding sun-dried tomatoes to a tomato sauce.

GARLIC-STUFFED LAMB

1½ pounds (trimmed weight) lamb loin, boned, fat and membranes removed (reserve tenderloins for another use, see Chef's Notes)

Oregano Marinade (page 48)

½ cup Roasted Garlic Paste (page 21)

Salt and freshly ground pepper

10 large Brussels sprouts, separated into leaves (save innermost leaves and core for another use)

2 tablespoons extra-virgin olive oil

6 ounces fresh wild or shiitake mushrooms, sliced ¼-inch thick

1 tablespoon finely chopped garlic

1 tablespoon finely chopped fresh thyme or 1 teaspoon dried thyme

1 cup lamb stock, chicken stock (page 42), or canned, low-salt chicken broth

3 tablespoons oregano olive oil (page 24)

¼ cup chopped fresh flat-leaf parsley

If buying fresh lamb, make a double batch and freeze half on the skewers. Convenience and compromise are cousins: Lamb is a meat that freezes very well. Make sure to transfer meat from the freezer to the refrigerator the day before you plan to serve it to ensure even thawing.

Slice lamb loin lengthwise (as if filleting) into 2 pieces about ½ inch thick. Using a mallet or the heel of your palm, lightly pound meat to about ¼-inch thickness, then cut each piece in half lengthwise. Place meat in a nonmetallic dish and pour marinade over the meat. Turn several times to coat, cover, and refrigerate at least 6 hours or overnight (see Chef's Notes). Turn meat occasionally in marinade.

When ready to cook, prepare grill or preheat broiler. Remove lamb from marinade and discard marinade. Spread about 1 tablespoon garlic paste on each of the lamb pieces. Season with salt and pepper. Roll meat lengthwise end to end and place on skewers. Grill or broil to desired doneness, 10 to 15 minutes for medium-rare meat, depending on heat of grill. Turn meat occasionally to ensure even cooking.

Meanwhile, bring a pot of salted water to a boil. Add Brussels sprout leaves and blanch 10 seconds. Immediately drain and spread on a baking sheet or in a large bowl to cool.

Heat extra-virgin olive oil in a large sauté pan over medium-high heat until almost smoking. Add mushrooms and do not move them for about 1 minute or until lightly brown on one side. Then sauté until brown, about 5 minutes. (It is very important that the mushrooms are not crowded, otherwise they will boil in their own juices rather than brown.)

Add garlic to sauté pan and continue to cook until golden brown, about 1 minute. Add thyme, then Brussels sprout leaves, and cook until leaves are wilted and bright green. Add stock and deglaze pan, scraping up all the loose bits on the bottom and edges of the pan. Simmer another 1 to 2 minutes. Add oregano olive oil and parsley. Season to taste with salt and pepper.

To serve, divide mushroom mixture among 4 hot plates and top with lamb. Spoon pan juices over.

VARIATION WITH SAUTÉED GARLIC: If you have not made garlic paste, simply sauté ½ cup finely chopped garlic in 2 tablespoons olive oil until light brown. Spread on the lamb and roll up.

VARIATION FOR MUSHROOM-STUFFED LAMB: You may also spread the sautéed mushrooms (omitting the Brussels sprout leaves) on the lamb and roll up. Make a sauce by reducing the stock by ½ and adding Brussels sprout leaves, oregano oil, and parsley.

Chef's Notes

Fresh lamb is typically sold bone in so when you ask your butcher to bone out the loin, you will get the tenderloin as well. If you purchase frozen lamb, usually the loin and tenderloin are sold separately. The lamb can marinate as little as 30 minutes if you are in a rush. Brush more marinade on the meat during cooking to add more flavor.

½ cup oregano olive oil
(page 24)

2 teaspoons finely
chopped garlic

½ teaspoon grated lemon zest

¼ teaspoon toasted red pepper
flakes (see Chef's Notes)
or 1 tablespoon pepper olive
oil (page 24)

Chef's Notes

Put red pepper flakes in a skillet and
heat over medium heat just until
flakes begin to brown. Immediately
remove from heat and pour onto a
cool dish to prevent burning.

OREGANO MARINADE

This is a great marinade for meat and poultry as well as for oily fish such as bluefish, tuna, mackerel, sardines, even swordfish. Lemon zest gives the flavor of lemon without the acidity of juice so you can give fish a lengthy soak. Don't be afraid of twelve hours for thick fillets or whole fish.

Put all ingredients in a bowl or jar and mix well. Keeps up to 4 days, refrigerated, in a tightly sealed container.

SUMMER/WINTER TOMATO SAUCE

Makes about 4 cups

This is a chunky, basic tomato sauce to use in lasagna, on pizza, or for pasta. And it can even be made into a soup (see variations). There was a time when fresh tomatoes contained lots of acidity and needed long cooking and/or the addition of a spoonful of sugar to balance the acid. Today, the acid has for the most part been bred out of tomatoes. The good news is that you can make tomato sauce in a short time, the bad news is that it can lack flavor. I add sun-dried tomatoes for extra flavor and work with local growers to grow antique tomato varieties that have the flavor I remember from childhood. You can grow your own tomatoes or shop at farmers' markets, where you are often allowed to taste before buying. Many markets now feature vine-ripened local tomatoes in season. Lacking tasty fresh tomatoes, use good-quality canned tomatoes.

Reserve juice from the chopped, fresh tomatoes by putting them in a strainer over a bowl. If using canned tomatoes, strain the juice from the tomatoes; reserve juice and chop tomatoes.

In a large, heavy saucepan, heat the extra-virgin olive oil over medium-high heat until hot. Add garlic and sauté until lightly browned. Add tomato juice and bay leaf and increase heat to high. Simmer until the juice has reduced by ⅓ for canned tomatoes and until it is thick for fresh tomatoes. Add tomato solids and sun-dried tomatoes and simmer until excess liquid has evaporated, 15 to 20 minutes. Season to taste with salt and pepper. Just before serving, swirl in butter and oregano oil.

VARIATION FOR A SMOOTH SAUCE: To make a rich, smooth sauce which really adheres to pasta, put sauce in blender and blend until smooth. With machine running, add another cup of extra-virgin olive oil. Try the sauce with ravioli and capellini.

VARIATION FOR TOMATO SOUP: Add 2 stalks celery (no leaves), chopped, and 1 medium onion, chopped, to the garlic and sauté until soft. Thin the sauce into a soup with chicken stock and finish with a little cream.

10 large tomatoes (about 4 pounds), peeled, seeded, and chopped or 2 cans (28 ounces each) high-quality plum (Roma) tomatoes

2 tablespoons extra-virgin olive oil

2 tablespoons finely chopped garlic

1 bay leaf

¼–½ cup chopped sun-dried tomatoes packed in oil (use larger amount with canned tomatoes or to enhance fresh tomatoes lacking in flavor)

Salt and freshly ground pepper

2 tablespoons unsalted butter

6 tablespoons oregano olive oil (page 24)

Chef's Notes

If not using the tomato sauce immediately, do not finish with the butter and oregano oil. During cooking and reheating, the butter and oil will separate from the sauce. Instead, wait until you plan to use the sauce, then finish with butter and oil.

4 ROSEMARY OLIVE OIL

Rosemary is another Mediterranean herb that often can be interchanged with basil and oregano. It has a strong, pungent, resinous character, which I like but some people may find overwhelming. Infusing it in oil smooths its flavor and allows it to mix easily with other flavors.

I particularly like rosemary for roasting potatoes, with eggplant, and with lamb. It has a particular affinity for fruit including grapes, pears, and oranges. (As an example, I have included a focaccia bread recipe here which includes raisins, fresh grapes, and lemon zest in the dough as well as baked on top. I have never been successful in keeping this bread from being devoured almost as soon as it has been cut into.)

For vegetables with strong flavors of their own, like artichokes and asparagus, rosemary makes a good match. Rosemary also works well with the saltiness of prosciutto as well as with fish with good flavor and meaty texture such as tuna.

ROSEMARY GRILLED AHI WITH ROASTED PEPPER SALAD

4 rosemary sprigs
(about 6 to 8 inches long)
or wood or metal skewers

4 center-cut ahi tuna steaks
(about 5 ounces each), cut
into blocks ¾ to 1 inch thick
and 3 inches long

¼ cup Rosemary and Roasted
Lemon Marinade (page 59)

Salt and freshly ground pepper

3 cups Roasted Pepper Salad
(facing page)

4 cups green salad (optional),
lightly dressed with Balsamic
Basil Vinaigrette (page 28)

I have a five-foot rosemary hedge outside my house from which I can cut long branches for skewers. The rosemary skewers make a dramatic presentation and add flavor; however, wooden and metal skewers will work nearly as well.

Soak rosemary or wooden skewers in water to cover 1 to 2 hours. Preheat grill or broiler. Skewer 2 tuna pieces lengthwise on each rosemary sprig and brush with marinade. Season with salt and pepper and grill, turning once or twice, to medium rare, 8 to 10 minutes, depending on heat.

Place a tuna skewer on each plate and top with ¾ cup Roasted Pepper Salad; make sure to spoon some juices from the salad over each serving. Garnish with green salad, if you like. Serve immediately.

ROASTED PEPPER SALAD —PEPPERONATA

Makes about 6 cups

I grew up on pepperonata served as a side dish with spiced flank steak. This is a very versatile salad: Serve it as a side vegetable, put it on pizza or in a crusty roll with arugula and slices of Italian cured meats. If you like spicy food, add a pinch of toasted, ground chili peppers.

Preheat broiler. Roast the peppers in the broiler or over an open flame or grill until skins are charred all over. Place in a plastic bag and close to steam the skins loose or use a bowl and lid. When cool, peel off the charred skins. Remove and discard core, seeds, and veins; reserve their juices. Cut the peppers into strips about ½ inch wide.

Place peppers and their juices in a mixing bowl and combine with the remaining ingredients. Adjust seasoning with salt and pepper. Let rest 30 minutes before serving. Salad keeps up to 4 days, refrigerated, in a tightly sealed container.

12 large red and yellow bell peppers (about 5 pounds)

½ cup peeled, seeded, and chopped vine-ripened, red tomatoes or good-quality canned, plum (Roma) tomatoes

1 tablespoon finely chopped garlic

¼ cup rinsed, drained, and roughly chopped capers

¼ cup finely chopped fresh flat-leaf parsley

2 tablespoons rosemary olive oil (page 24)

6 tablespoons extra-virgin olive oil

3 tablespoons champagne wine vinegar or white wine vinegar

¼ cup pitted ripe olives (such as Kalamata)

Salt and freshly ground pepper

Chef's Notes

Roasted garlic olive oil may be substituted for rosemary olive oil or use a tablespoon of each.

HARVEST FOCACCIA

Makes 3 pounds dough; enough for 1
standard, 11 x 17-inch baking sheet

1 ounce fresh yeast
or 2 envelopes active dry yeast

2 cups lukewarm whole milk

1 tablespoon
plus 1 teaspoon sugar

5 cups all-purpose flour
plus more for sprinkling
the work surface

⅓ (about) cup rosemary
olive oil (page 24)

1 tablespoon finely chopped
fresh rosemary (optional)

1 teaspoon grated lemon zest

1 cup halved or quartered
red grapes

1 cup golden raisins

1½ teaspoons salt

1 whole egg, beaten
with a fork until frothy

Coarse salt

Chef's Notes

Dough may also be cut and
shaped into three 1-pound pieces.
Each piece can be shaped into
a 10-inch round.

In Tuscany, this bread was traditionally made on the first day of harvest as a snack for the field workers with this year's grapes and the raisins of the previous harvest. Serve it for breakfast, as a *spuntino* (midday snack), as part of an antipasto with prosciutto, or with cheeses as a cheese course. The recipe makes a soft, tender, and delicious bread blending sweet and savory flavors. The recipe may be doubled if your mixer will hold ten cups of flour.

In a large bowl or the work bowl of an electric mixer, dissolve yeast in lukewarm milk and add 1 tablespoon sugar and 1 cup of the flour. Mix well and let stand in a warm place about 15 minutes for the yeast to activate.

In a small saucepan, warm ¼ cup of the rosemary oil with chopped rosemary (if using) and lemon zest. Add grapes and raisins, mix well, and add ½ to yeast mixture. Mix another 1 cup flour into yeast mixture with the dough hook attachment. Knead until smooth. With machine running, add salt and remaining 3 cups flour, 1 cup at a time, kneading until smooth after each addition. Knead another 6 minutes after final addition of flour. The dough should remain rather wet to ensure a soft and light bread. Shape dough into a ball on a floured board and put in an oiled bowl. Cover with a damp towel and allow to rise in a warm place until doubled in bulk, about 45 minutes.

Punch dough down and lightly sprinkle work surface with flour. Turn out dough and knead lightly. At this point, dough may be wrapped and frozen.

If ready to bake, preheat oven to 400 degrees F. Oil a baking sheet. Press dough down into a flat disc with the heel of your hand. (Dough is pliable and easy to work.) Using your fingertips, nudge the dough into a rectangle. Stretch and pull the dough and nudge it into shape to fit a cookie sheet. Dough can be rolled but the pressure will produce a heavier bread; the irregularities of hand shaping are part of the bread's charm. Transfer dough to oiled baking sheet and brush with 2 tablespoons rosemary oil. Let rise again in a warm place until doubled, 30 to 40 minutes.

Make indentations all over the dough by pressing with your fingertips, being careful not to puncture all the way through the dough. Bake 15 minutes, remove from oven, and brush with beaten egg. Sprinkle with remaining 1 teaspoon sugar and spread with remaining rosemary oil-grape mixture and a light sprinkling of coarse salt. Return to oven and continue to bake until golden brown on top and crisp on the bottom, about 10 minutes. Let cool in pan to room temperature before cutting.

VARIATION FOR BREAD STICKS: The same dough may be used to make bread sticks. Cut off 2-ounce portions of dough and roll under the palms of your hands into long rolls. Their irregularities are part of their charm. Brush with flavored or plain olive oil and roll in seeds such as poppy, sesame, or fennel or a mixture of all, if desired. Transfer to an oiled cookie sheet and let rise in a warm place until doubled in bulk, about 15 minutes. Bake in a preheated 400 degree F oven until golden brown, about 15 minutes.

½ cup chicken stock
(page 42) or canned low-salt
chicken broth

1½ cups Rosemary-Roasted
Eggplant Paste (see below)

Salt and freshly ground pepper

1 pound dried pasta
(shape of your choice)

3 cups loosely packed arugula or baby spinach, roughly
chopped if leaves are large

¼ cup finely chopped fresh
flat-leaf parsley

1 cup freshly grated
Parmesan cheese

PASTA WITH ROASTED EGGPLANT SAUCE

Serves 4 to 6

This is a very quick, simple, homey pasta. It is very Italian in that the sauce coats the pasta without a pool of extra sauce. It may not be very colorful, but it tastes great.

In a medium saucepan, bring stock to a boil over medium-high heat. Lower heat to medium and whisk in eggplant paste. Adjust seasoning with salt and pepper to taste.

Meanwhile, cook pasta until al dente in lots of boiling, salted water. When cooked, drain well, reserving ½ cup of the cooking liquid, and immediately return pasta to the cooking pot. Add arugula to pasta and toss so arugula begins to heat and wilt. Add eggplant mixture and parsley and mix well. Add some of the reserved pasta cooking liquid if sauce seems too thick.

Pour onto a heated platter or serving bowl or divide among 4 to 6 hot bowls. Sprinkle with Parmesan and serve.

---

1 large eggplant
(about 1½ pounds)

4 tablespoons extra-virgin
olive oil

½ tablespoon rosemary
olive oil (page 24)

½ tablespoon roasted garlic
oil or 2 tablespoons Roasted
Garlic Paste (page 21)

Salt and freshly ground pepper

ROSEMARY-ROASTED EGGPLANT PASTE

Makes 1 to 1½ cups

This simple dish makes a great appetizer spread on bread, a sauce for a tomatoless pizza, or a dip for vegetables. It also makes a delicious, easy pasta sauce when thinned with vegetable or chicken stock (page 42). The blacker the eggplant gets during roasting, the smokier the flavor becomes.

Preheat broiler and set rack to low. Use your hands to lightly oil eggplant with 1 tablespoon of the extra-virgin olive oil and place on a baking sheet. Roast, turning occasionally, until very soft and black, about 45 minutes. Set aside to cool.

Scrape eggplant pulp into the work bowl of a food processor. If seeds are large, cut out and discard. Process until smooth. Add flavored oils and remaining 3 tablespoons extra-virgin olive oil and process again. Season with salt and pepper to taste. Keeps up to 4 days refrigerated in a tightly sealed container.

SHAVED ARTICHOKE
AND ASPARAGUS SALAD

Serves 6

This spring I was inspired by the beautiful artichokes in the markets to create a new, raw artichoke salad. It can be turned into a main dish salad with the addition of a piece of sautéed or roasted fish, such as halibut.

Bring a large pot of salted water to a boil. Cut off and discard the top third of the artichokes. Snap off the dark, outer leaves until only the pale, yellow-green leaves remain. Cut off all but 1 inch of the stem. With a paring knife, trim artichokes and their stems of all remaining dark green parts. Cut in half lengthwise through the hearts and remove fuzzy chokes with a spoon. Slice halves lengthwise very thinly and put in a bowl of water with 2 tablespoons of the lemon juice.

When the salted water boils, add asparagus and blanch until just tender, about 5 minutes. Immediately drain and plunge into a bowl of ice water. Drain again. Drain artichokes well and put in a bowl with the remaining lemon juice, olive oils, and parsley. Season with salt and pepper. Toss well. Moisten asparagus with some of the dressing.

To serve, mound a portion of artichoke salad on each of 6 plates and top each with 3 asparagus spears. With a vegetable peeler, shave strips of Parmesan or pecorino over the top and serve.

VARIATION WITH GRILLED ASPARAGUS: Blanch asparagus 2 to 3 minutes or until slightly undercooked. Brush with a tablespoon rosemary oil and grill until tender, turning occasionally to ensure even cooking, 2 to 3 minutes.

8 medium-sized artichokes

½ cup fresh lemon juice
(preferably from Meyer lemons)

18 spears asparagus,
trimmed and ends peeled

¼ cup rosemary olive oil
(page 24)

1 cup extra-virgin olive oil

2 tablespoons chopped
fresh flat-leaf parsley

Salt and freshly ground pepper

2 ounces Parmesan
or pecorino cheese

1 pound fresh fava beans,
black-eyed peas, or lima beans

1 pound fresh peas
(about 10 ounces shelled)

1 zucchini (½ pound),
cut into ¼-inch dice

2 ears corn, kernels cut
off the cob

¼ pound prosciutto,
cut into paper-thin slices

1 teaspoon grated lemon zest

3 cups cooked long-grain
white rice

¼ cup rosemary olive oil
(page 24)

¼ cup extra-virgin olive oil

¼ cup fresh lemon juice

2 tablespoons chopped fresh
flat-leaf parsley

1 small red onion,
cut into ¼-inch dice

Salt and freshly ground pepper

SPRING VEGETABLE RICE SALAD WITH ROSEMARY-LEMON VINAIGRETTE

This is really a vegetable salad with rice. Feel free to substitute any of your favorite vegetables or whatever is abundant in your garden, such as tomatoes, eggplant, bell peppers, and green beans.

Bring a large pot of salted water to a boil. Blanch the vegetables, one at a time, until they are just tender. As they are cooked, drain and spread them out on a cookie sheet to cool (see Chef's Notes). When cool, peel fava beans and mix with other vegetables in a serving bowl. Cut half of the prosciutto into julienne and add it to the vegetables with the lemon zest and rice. Toss well.

For the dressing, mix together in a bowl or jar the rosemary and extra-virgin olive oils, lemon juice, parsley, red onion, and salt and pepper to taste. Let sit at least 10 minutes before mixing with the salad.

When ready to serve, whisk dressing well again; then pour over the salad and toss well. Adjust seasoning. Arrange salad on 6 chilled plates. Lay 2 slices prosciutto over half of each salad and serve.

Chef's Notes

I do not use an ice bath to stop further cooking of blanched vegetables unless I have to (for instance, for asparagus) but prefer to pan shock vegetables, spreading them on a baking sheet to cool. To preserve vitamins and minerals, you might want to cook the rice in the vegetable cooking water. Just remember to measure the water to make sure there is enough to cook the rice. Add more boiling water if necessary.

ROSEMARY MARINADE

Makes about 1 cup

Rosemary marinade is delicious brushed on meat and poultry such as lamb, chicken, turkey, and veal before and during cooking. It gives a wonderful flavor to grilled vegetables such as radicchio, peppers, eggplant, and zucchini. The marinade may also be simply drizzled over a finished dish as a sauce.

Combine anchovy fillets, garlic, and capers in a mixing bowl. Mix well. Whisk in red wine vinegar. Slowly add rosemary oil and extra-virgin olive oil, while whisking, to form an emulsion. Add parsley and pepper to taste. (The marinade may also be made in a blender or food processor.) Keeps up to 1 week refrigerated in a tightly sealed container.

VARIATION WITH GRILLED RADICCHIO: Cut each whole radicchio head into 4 wedges. Lightly coat with marinade and grill over medium heat until tender. Drizzle with more marinade before serving. Serve as a side dish.

10 oil-packed anchovy fillets, well drained and minced

2 teaspoons finely chopped garlic

2 teaspoons capers, rinsed, drained, and chopped if large

¼ cup red wine vinegar

½ cup rosemary olive oil (page 24)

½ cup extra-virgin olive oil

2 teaspoons finely chopped fresh flat-leaf parsley

Freshly ground pepper to taste

ROSEMARY AND ROASTED LEMON MARINADE

Makes about 1 ½ cups

By roasting the lemons, their acidity mellows considerably. We often use this technique when creating wine dinners so the food will not conflict with the wines.

Preheat broiler. Place lemons, cut side up, in a small, nonaluminum baking dish and sprinkle with salt and pepper. Roast, about 6 inches below the heat, until very soft, about 20 minutes. The tops will darken and caramelize. Let cool in the baking dish.

Squeeze the lemon pulp and juice and scrape all the cooking juices from the baking dish into a strainer supported over a bowl. Force it through and add garlic. Whisk in rosemary oil and extra-virgin olive oil. Keeps up to 1 week refrigerated in a tightly sealed container.

To marinate: Lightly coat chicken pieces or whole birds with marinade, cover with plastic wrap, and let stand, refrigerated, 24 hours. Marinate fish for 12 hours.

6 lemons, cut in half

Salt and freshly ground pepper

2 teaspoons finely chopped garlic

⅔ cup rosemary olive oil (page 24)

⅓ cup extra-virgin olive oil

5 ROASTED GARLIC OLIVE OIL

Roasted garlic olive oil is the second oil I made after basil; it and the basil oil are still my favorite flavors. I sauté garlic until pale gold or roast whole heads to make a paste. Using roasted garlic oil means you can achieve the same flavor without the fuss and mess!

While I prefer the taste of cooked garlic to raw, a garlic oil flavored with raw garlic can be readily substituted in any of the recipes. A spoonful or two of roasted garlic paste will also achieve a similar effect as the oil. Because the garlic in roasted garlic oil is already a cooked, caramelized flavor, you can sauté in a roasted garlic oil without much loss of the garlicky flavor.

The taste of a raw garlic oil will change if subjected to heat.

Roasted garlic oil is one of the most versatile flavored olives oils. Use it to sauté vegetables such as sliced asparagus. Topped with a few toasted, chopped almonds, you will have created a dish fit for company or even, with a piece of Parmesan cheese and bread, a weeknight supper.

Use roasted garlic oil as a base to flavor grains and pasta dishes. In fact, it can be a pasta sauce on its own with the addition of chopped parsley, grated cheese, and salt and pepper.

4 slices bacon, diced

¼ cup roasted garlic olive oil
(page 21)

2 bunches fresh spinach,
washed and dried

Salt and freshly ground pepper

SAUTÉED SPINACH

Roasted garlic oil does wonderful things for vegetables so easily! A simple vegetable dish becomes suddenly exciting. Try sautéing English and sugar snap peas, asparagus cut in rounds on the diagonal, arugula, kale, even red bell peppers.

In a large sauté pan, slowly cook bacon until crisp. Remove bacon and drain on paper towel. Pour off fat from the pan and add garlic oil. Heat over medium-high heat. Add spinach and sauté quickly until wilted and dry. Season with salt and pepper and serve.

VARIATION WITH PASTA: For a light, quick entrée, toss the spinach with ½ pound pasta, cooked al dente, and ¼ to ½ cup freshly grated Parmesan cheese.

---

6 tablespoons roasted garlic
olive oil (page 21)

1⅓ pounds large shrimp with
shells, peeled and deveined

Salt and freshly ground pepper

½ cup dry white wine

1 tablespoon fresh lemon juice

1 large vine-ripened tomato,
peeled, seeded, and chopped

¼ cup finely chopped fresh
flat-leaf parsley

2 bunches arugula

WARM SHRIMP
AND ARUGULA SALAD

Serves 4 as an entrée;
6 to 8 as an appetizer

This adaptation of a slow, oven method for cooking fish was taught to me by Lydia Bastianich of Delidia Restaurant in Manhattan. It gives very tender results, especially important if you are using frozen shrimp! Here, I use it for shrimp but I also use if for oysters, clams, scallops, and squid. While the recipe can be completed on top of the stove, I find it easier to put the fish in the oven as described here; this frees the cook for several minutes for other tasks.

Preheat oven to 300 degrees F. Heat 3 tablespoons of the garlic oil in a large, oven-going sauté pan until very hot over medium heat. Season shrimp with salt and pepper and add to pan. Cook over low heat for a few seconds, just until shrimp begin to give up their juices. Add white wine and immediately put pan in preheated oven 2 to 4 minutes or until fish is just cooked. Do not overcook!

Remove shrimp to a bowl with a slotted spoon. Add lemon juice to cooking liquids in sauté pan and boil rapidly until reduced by half. Remove pan from heat and immediately add remaining 3 tablespoons oil, tomato, parsley, arugula, and shrimp. Toss well. Shrimp should be just barely warm and arugula barely wilted.

ROASTED GARLIC
AND PORCINI MARINADE

Makes about ½ cup

This has a robust flavor, great for meats with lots of flavor such as beef, lamb, and pork. Use for a crown roast of pork or simply brush on one side of a steak, grill, turn, and brush the second side.

Place marinade ingredients in a blender or food processor and blend until smooth. Brush on meats before cooking; baste occasionally during cooking with more marinade.

2 teaspoons Dijon mustard

2 tablespoons roasted garlic olive oil (page 21)

2 tablespoons porcini olive oil (page 24)

½ teaspoon chopped fresh thyme or pinch dried thyme

½ teaspoon chopped fresh oregano or pinch dried oregano

1½ tablespoons fresh lemon juice

½ teaspoon red pepper flakes

½ teaspoon freshly ground pepper

ROASTED GARLIC CAESAR SALAD

Serves 3 to 4;
makes about 1 ¼ cups dressing

8 anchovy fillets, drained well

1 tablespoon Dijon mustard

2 tablespoons fresh lemon juice

1 tablespoon champagne wine vinegar or white wine vinegar

Freshly ground pepper

1 egg yolk

Dash Worcestershire sauce

1¼ cups roasted garlic olive oil (page 21)

1 cup freshly grated Parmesan cheese

2–3 heads romaine lettuce

Garlic croutons (see Chef's Notes)

Chef's Notes

Easy croutons: Preheat oven to 350 degrees F. Cut four ½-inch-thick slices of country bread (including crusts) into small cubes. Toss with 1 tablespoon garlic oil and season with salt and pepper. Bake about 10 minutes or until toasted with a little softness left in the center.

Caesar salad dressing may also be used as a dip for vegetables or as a spread for sandwiches such as roasted or grilled vegetables and chicken. Depending on how richly you like your salad dressed, use about three-fourths of the dressing for the salad and keep the rest on hand. Or forget salad entirely and use the dressing to sauce baked potatoes instead! If you are concerned about using raw eggs, see variation at end of recipe.

Combine anchovies, mustard, lemon juice, vinegar, pepper, egg yolk, and Worcestershire sauce in a blender or food processor. Blend until smooth. With machine running, slowly add roasted garlic oil to form an emulsion. Thin, if necessary, with warm water. Add ½ cup Parmesan and mix in with a few brief pulses. Adjust seasoning. Sauce can be made up to 2 days ahead. Refrigerate in a tightly covered container.

To make the salad, remove outer leaves of romaine until remaining are firm and pale green. Separate into leaves and put into a salad bowl. Pour about ¾ of the dressing over the lettuce, add garlic croutons, and toss well. Pass the remaining Parmesan at table.

VARIATION WITH PASTEURIZED LIQUID EGGS AND CHOLESTEROL-FREE LIQUID EGGS: Follow directions on the package and use the equivalent of 1 whole egg for the mayonnaise recipes in this book. Cholesterol-free liquid eggs, such as Egg Beaters, are readily available and work for these recipes as well. Use ¼ cup liquid egg and 1 tablespoon vinegar or lemon juice and proceed with the recipe as written. The texture is very light but the emulsion does not break and it tastes very good. There is the added benefit of enjoying mayonnaise without fear of cholesterol!

GRILLED STEAK
WITH GARLIC SMASHED POTATOES

2 pounds flank steak
(or other preferred cut,
such as London Broil)

Roasted Garlic and
Porcini Marinade (page 63)

Salt and freshly ground pepper

2 tablespoons roasted garlic
olive oil (page 21)

3 tablespoons porcini olive oil
(page 24)

Garlic Smashed Potatoes
(facing page)

Chef's Notes

Remember to oil your grill well
to prevent sticking, or invest in a
nonstick or cast iron insert.
The steak can be cooked immediately upon being coated with marinade if you are rushed. There will be
a little less flavor than if
given a longer time to marinate.

I gave some flavored oils to Mike Moone when we were considering our joint venture, Napa Valley Kitchens, producers of specialty foods. He used them that night on a barbecued steak and called me the next morning to seal our deal. This is an adaptation of his recipe. The combination of porcini and garlic oil gives a deep, sweet, earthy flavor, soylike without the saltiness.

Flank steak tends to curl on a barbecue. To prevent this, prick the steak all over with the point of a knife. This will tenderize the meat, allow the marinade to penetrate more readily, and prevent the meat from curling on the grill.

Pour marinade over the steak in a nonaluminum dish. Turn meat several times to coat evenly with marinade. Cover and refrigerate 2 hours or overnight (see Chef's Notes). Turn occasionally.

When ready to cook, preheat grill or broiler. Season steak with salt and pepper on both sides and grill or broil to desired doneness, 7 to 10 minutes for medium rare, depending on heat of the grill. When done, remove meat to a heated platter and drizzle the garlic and porcini oils over the steak. Let rest 5 to 6 minutes. Slice steak thinly, reserving juices in the platter. To serve, place the sliced meat over the hot smashed potatoes and pour the juices over all.

GARLIC SMASHED POTATOES

Serves 4

This is it—the mashed potato recipe you will use for the rest of your culinary life! I occasionally use the same recipe for sweet potatoes. Make more potatoes than you think you need. They will all disappear!

Cook potatoes in a large pot of boiling, salted water until fork tender. Drain well and let dry on a baking pan 5 minutes.

In a large bowl, begin mashing the potatoes with the butter using an electric mixer. Heat cream to a boil, add to potatoes, and continue to beat. Add garlic oil and beat again. Season with salt and pepper to taste. Beat in chives. If too thick, thin with warm milk. Reheat, if necessary (this is most easily done in a microwave oven).

VARIATION WITH OTHER VEGETABLES: Feel free to add other vegetable purées to the potatoes such as asparagus or roasted peppers. Depending on the moistness of the added vegetable purée, you can use up to equal proportions of each. If the result is too wet, simply stir it over heat in a pot until it reaches its desired consistency.

2 pounds baking potatoes, peeled and cut into large chunks

1 tablespoon unsalted butter

½ cup heavy cream

½ cup roasted garlic olive oil (page 21)

Salt and freshly ground pepper

2 tablespoons chopped fresh chives

Chef's Notes

If you love garlic, the potatoes will easily absorb more garlic oil, up to another ½ cup. The result is a luxuriously smooth purée redolent of roast garlic.

SPAGHETTINI
WITH ROASTED GARLIC OIL

Serves 4 to 6

Without a doubt, this is my favorite late-night pasta. Not only is it easy to digest, it is very quickly cooked and even easier to clean up!

Bring a large pot of salted water to a vigorous boil and add pasta a handful at a time so water stays at a boil. Cook until al dente, 7 to 8 minutes.

While pasta is cooking, warm ¼ cup of the roasted garlic oil with the chili flakes in a large saucepan over medium heat. Heat just until chili flakes begin to move and sizzle.

When pasta is done, drain well and toss in the saucepan with the oil and chili flakes. Add stock and season with salt and pepper. Add remaining ½ cup oil, ¾ cup of the cheese, and the parsley and toss again. Serve immediately in warmed bowls, topped with remaining cheese.

1 pound dried spaghettini

¾ cup roasted garlic olive oil (page 21)

½ teaspoon chili flakes

½ cup chicken stock (page 42) or canned, low-salt chicken broth or pasta cooking liquid

Salt and freshly ground pepper

1 cup freshly grated Parmesan cheese

3 tablespoons finely chopped fresh flat-leaf parsley

6 PEPPER OLIVE OIL

There are many pepper and chili oils on the market. Some have dried chilies in the bottle; some have a blend of chilies, black pepper, and herbs. Each will have its own flavor and degree of heat. With the exception of Chinese chili oils, which are fiery hot, any of the pepper oils will work with these recipes. However, I recommend you taste your oil—commercial or homemade—to determine its heat before starting a preparation, then adjust the amount you use.

Pepper oils may be used for sautéing and roasting without great loss of flavor; however, the subtleties of flavor in fresh, uncooked chilies or bell peppers may be lost with high-heat cooking. Eggs—from simple fried eggs to omelets—are terrific cooked in pepper oil. Seafood, too, including shrimp and scallops, is delicious cooked with pepper oil. Pepper oil is a natural for any dish with a Southwestern bent. And try popcorn with pepper oil!

SCRAMBLED EGGS with PEPPER OIL

Serves 4

4 tablespoons pepper olive oil (page 24)

1 tablespoon finely chopped garlic

4 slices crusty Italian bread

8 eggs

2 tablespoons cream or milk

½ tablespoon chopped fresh oregano or 1 teaspoon dried oregano

Salt and freshly ground pepper

Eggs scrambled slowly over low heat are always welcome for a leisurely breakfast. When the eggs are scrambled in pepper oil, the taste is both comforting and invigorating! Make them for supper and serve with a simple green salad.

Heat 2 tablespoons of the pepper oil in a nonstick skillet over medium heat. Add garlic and cook gently until transparent, about 3 minutes. Let cool a minute or two, then brush garlic and oil on one side of the bread. Toast or grill bread and keep warm.

Heat remaining 2 tablespoons oil in the same pan over medium-low heat. Break eggs into a mixing bowl, add cream or milk, and oregano, and season with salt and pepper. Mix well with a fork or whisk. Pour into the heated pan and cook slowly, folding the eggs over themselves until cooked to desired degree. Put a garlic toast on each of 4 plates and spoon eggs over.

GRILLED CHICKEN SALAD SANDWICH

Makes 4 sandwiches

1 whole, large chicken breast, boned, skin on

Salt and freshly ground pepper

¼ cup finely chopped onion

2 tablespoons finely chopped carrot

2 tablespoons finely chopped celery

1 tablespoon finely chopped fresh flat-leaf parsley

1 tablespoon finely chopped fresh oregano

¾ cup Pepper Aioli (page 74)

1 tablespoon milk or buttermilk (optional)

8 slices toasted or grilled crusty Italian bread

Crisp lettuce (such as iceberg, butter, or bibb)

The color of the pepper aioli turns the salad a pretty salmon pink color. The proportions make a crunchy salad; if you prefer more meat to vegetables, add another chicken breast.

Preheat grill or broiler. Season chicken on both sides with salt and pepper and grill until done, about 7 minutes. Let cool. Discard skin and cut meat into large dice. Put in a mixing bowl.

Add onion, carrot, celery, parsley, and oregano. Mix in pepper aioli. Season with salt and pepper to taste. If salad is too thick, thin with milk or buttermilk. Spread a little of the salad on each slice of bread. Top 4 slices with lettuce, top with second slice, and press down. Slice in half diagonally.

BRODETTO OF MANILA CLAMS AND DRIED SAUSAGE

Serves 4

This brodetto (seafood broth) is a typical southern Italian fisherman's lunch. He would take along with him bread, dried sausage, and white or red wine. The seafood he would add from his catch. I like to use a baguette studded with olives but a plain baguette will do very well. This recipe is also delicious as a pasta sauce.

Scrub clams very well in fresh water. Discard any that are open and do not close when poked. Let soak in cold water until ready to use.

Preheat oven to 425 degrees F. Heat butter over medium heat in a large, oven-going sauté pan until butter turns a light brown. Add baguette pieces and toss to coat all over with butter. Put in oven and bake until crust is brown and well developed, about 10 minutes. Turn, if necessary, to brown evenly all over. Drain on paper towels and keep warm.

Heat pepper oil in a sauté pan over medium-high heat until hot. Add garlic and sauté until garlic is lightly brown, 10 to 15 seconds. Regulate heat by moving the pan on and off the heat.

Add clams to sauté pan and stir well. Add white wine, turn heat to high, and cook, stirring the clams occasionally, until they have popped open, about 5 minutes. Add sausage halfway through the cooking. Discard any clams that remain closed. Simmer rapidly until liquid has reduced by half. Season with salt and pepper. Add chopped parsley and mix well. Put one toasted baguette piece, cut side up, in each soup plate and pour clam mixture over.

Serve immediately.

VARIATION WITH MUSSELS: You can use mussels instead of clams and spicy Italian sausage (just remember to cook and drain the sausage first).

1½ pounds medium-sized manila clams in shells

2 tablespoons butter

4 pieces baguette (each 2 to 3 inches long)

3 tablespoons pepper olive oil (page 24)

2 tablespoons thinly sliced garlic

1 cup dry white wine

⅓ pound spicy, dry sausage, cut into ⅓-inch dice

Salt and freshly ground pepper

¼ cup finely chopped fresh flat-leaf parsley

3 cups vine-ripened plum
(Roma) tomatoes, cored and
cut into thin wedges

Salt and freshly ground pepper

1 tablespoon finely chopped
fresh oregano or 1 teaspoon
dried oregano

1 tablespoon finely chopped
fresh flat-leaf parsley

1 tablespoon minced garlic

¼ cup minced red onion

2 tablespoons rinsed, drained,
and roughly chopped capers

½ cup roasted, seeded, and
coarsely chopped red or yellow
bell pepper (page 184)

12 pitted and sliced
Greek olives (such as Kalamata
or Gaeta olives)

2 tablespoons fresh lemon juice

2 tablespoons pepper olive oil
(page 24)

6 tablespoons extra-virgin
olive oil

½ pound dried linguini

4 large sheets parchment paper
or waxed paper
(see Chef's Notes)

4 swordfish steaks
(5 ounces each)

SWORDFISH with MEDITERRANEAN TOMATO SAUCE and LINGUINI

Serves 4;
makes about 1 quart sauce

This recipe is an adaptation of a fresh Mediterranean tomato sauce from Carol Dearth, who currently lives in the Pacific Northwest. Carol, who lived in Naples for two years, credits the Italians with teaching her the importance of using very, very fresh ingredients and treating them simply and intelligently. The recipe makes more tomato sauce than you will need for the fish. It is delicious as a pasta sauce, a topping for bruschetta, or a sauce or side dish for grilled poultry or meat. For the best flavor, use garden fresh tomatoes.

Put tomatoes in a large bowl and season with salt and pepper to taste. Add oregano, parsley, garlic, onion, capers, peppers, olives, lemon juice, pepper oil, and 4 tablespoons of the extra-virgin olive oil. Stir gently just to mix and set aside at least 1 hour. Adjust seasonings if desired. Mixture will become more liquid and saucelike over time.

Preheat oven to 450 degrees F. Bring a large pot of salted water to a boil and cook linguini until al dente. Drain and toss with remaining 2 tablespoons extra-virgin olive oil. Reserve.

Fold 4 large sheets of parchment paper in half. With the fold as the spine, cut a large semicircle (about an 8-inch radius) with one end more pointed than the other (opened out, the shape resembles a heart). Open the circles and arrange a small pile of linguini in the center of one side of each of the 4 sheets. Top with a spoonful of tomato sauce, making sure to moisten the linguini with the juices. Lay a piece of fish on top and arrange with another spoonful of sauce. Moisten again with juices from the sauce and season with salt and pepper. Leave a 1-inch border of paper clear.

Close the parchment over the fish. Starting at the flatter end of the semicircle, firmly fold the edge inwards. Fold entire edge into a series of tight, flat, overlapping pleats to enclose the fish. Fold the last pleat several times and tuck it under the bag. Put the bags on a baking sheet and bake in the oven 12 to 15 minutes. The bags will puff up and brown. To serve, transfer the bags to 4 warmed dinner plates and let each diner cut open the package to enjoy the aromas.

Chef's Notes
Waxed paper is a nice touch to make the cooking bags because you
can see the colors of the sauce through it.

2 garlic cloves, finely chopped

1 egg yolk

1 tablespoon fresh lemon juice

¾ cup pepper olive oil
(page 24) or half pepper olive
oil and half olive oil

Salt and freshly ground pepper

¼ cup fine, dried white
bread crumbs

 # PEPPER AIOLI

The bread crumbs give the sauce a completely different texture: less oily, lighter. They also prevent the sauce from separating when adding it to hot soups, for instance. Use this aioli as a sandwich spread, to enrich a fish soup, to perk up a grilled chicken breast, and to spoon over a broiled steak. It is also delicious with any kind of shellfish. If you are concerned about using raw eggs, see variation at end of recipe.

Put garlic, egg yolk, and lemon juice in a food processor or blender and process. With machine running, add pepper oil drop by drop until an emulsion forms, then pour in a slow steady stream. Thin, if necessary, with a tablespoon warm water. Season to taste with salt and pepper and pulse in bread crumbs.

CITRUS OIL VARIATION: Make the sauce with citrus oil instead of pepper oil and serve with Marinated Grilled Shrimp Cocktail, page 88.

VARIATION WITH PASTEURIZED LIQUID EGGS AND CHOLESTEROL-FREE LIQUID EGGS: Follow directions on the package and use the equivalent of 1 whole egg for the mayonnaise recipes in this book. Cholesterol-free liquid eggs, such as Egg Beaters, are readily available and work for these recipes as well. Use ¼ cup liquid egg and 1 tablespoon vinegar or lemon juice and proceed with the recipe as written. The texture is very light but the emulsion does not break and it tastes very good. There is the added benefit of enjoying mayonnaise without fear of cholesterol!

PASTINA RISOTTO
WITH ROASTED PEPPERS AND BROCCOLI

This dish was inspired by Nick Morfogen. He was my executive sous-chef at Tra Vigne until 1993 when we opened Ajax Mountain Tavern in Aspen, Colorado, and made him chef and partner in the new venture. Pastina is the most comforting of all pastas for Italians to eat because it is the pasta of childhood. Pastina is the diminutive form of the word *pasta*. And pastina is exactly that—tiny grains of pasta that look more like a cooked grain than a pasta. This dish can be varied according to the season by adding whatever vegetables are best: Peas and asparagus are two of my favorites.

Bring a large pot of salted water to a boil. Add pastina and cook until it is slightly undercooked, about 11 minutes. Make sure to stir occasionally during cooking or the pasta will stick to the bottom of the pan. Drain pasta and run under cold water to stop the cooking. Drain again and reserve.

Heat oil in a saucepan over medium-high heat until hot. Add garlic and cook until light brown, moving pan on and off heat as necessary to regulate temperature. Add broccoli and cook until it turns bright green, about 1 minute. Season with salt and pepper. Add thyme; it should make a crackling sound as it hits the hot pan.

Add stock to broccoli mixture and bring to a boil over high heat. Boil until reduced by half. Add peppers and cooked pastina and return mixture to a boil. Stir in ¾ cup of the Parmesan and season with salt and pepper. Swirl in butter, if desired, for a richer-tasting dish. Pour into a heated serving bowl or individual soup plates and sprinkle with remaining ¼ cup cheese.

1 pound dried pastina
(#78 Acini di Pepe)

5 tablespoons pepper olive oil
(page 24)

2 tablespoons chopped garlic

3 cups broccoli florets

Salt and freshly ground pepper

2 tablespoons chopped
fresh thyme

3 cups hot chicken stock
(page 42) or canned,
low-salt chicken broth
or vegetable broth

3 red bell peppers, roasted,
peeled, seeded, and cut into
½-inch dice (page 184)

1 cup freshly grated
Parmesan cheese

½ stick (4 tablespoons) butter
(optional)

Chef's Notes

The preparation of this dish resembles that for risotto, thus the name, but it takes less time and can be prepared ahead of time without loss of quality: Follow the recipe through the reduction of the stock. Reserve the pasta and broth separately, then assemble the dish in minutes when ready to serve.

7 PORCINI OLIVE OIL

Fresh, wild mushrooms, especially porcini, can often run up to twenty-five dollars a pound when you can find them. Shiitakes are being grown commercially and so are more available and less expensive but still cost an average of twelve to fifteen dollars per pound. By using a mushroom-infused oil such as porcini olive oil combined with domestic mushrooms in a dish calling for wild mushrooms, you can achieve much of the same flavor as wild mushrooms more economically.

One of the great pleasures of cooking occurs when an experiment turns out far better than you expected. Such is the case with cooking with porcini oil. It takes on a sweet, earthy flavor which took me completely by surprise. This oil can add a meaty flavor to vegetarian dishes, one of the hardest things to do. Porcini oil is also a wonderful complementary flavor with pancetta and pork as well as dried fruits. Porcini oil works with any food you might imagine good with mushrooms, such as beef and lamb.

¼ pound pancetta, cut into
¼-inch dice

4 tablespoons porcini olive oil
(page 24)

2 tablespoons chopped garlic

1 tablespoon chopped
fresh thyme

⅓ cup sherry vinegar

¼ cup dried cherries

5 ounces fresh goat cheese

6 cups mixed greens,
such as frisée (curly endive)
and baby spinach

Salt and freshly ground pepper

WARM GOAT CHEESE
AND PANCETTA SALAD

I created this recipe for my friend, goat cheese maker Laura Chenel, years ago. It really is a winter salad, but we love it so much that we make it year round by varying the fruits and greens according to the season: Instead of cherries, we have served the salad with cherry tomatoes, grilled, sliced pears, and grilled or chopped oven-dried figs. The salad makes a festive, seasonal supper with a glass of Beaujolais nouveau and crusty bread.

Render diced pancetta in a small sauté pan over low heat until pancetta has released its fat and the meat has lightly browned all over. Drain pancetta on paper towels and reserve 1 tablespoon of the fat in the pan.

Add 2 tablespoons of the porcini oil to the pan and heat over medium-high heat. Return pancetta to pan and cook until crispy. Add garlic and sauté until light brown. Remove pan from heat, add thyme, and stir well. Add vinegar, return pan to heat, and deglaze pan, scraping up all the brown bits that cling to the bottom and sides of the pan. Add cherries and simmer until reduced by half.

Off the heat, crumble the goat cheese into the pan and stir to break up the cheese. Add the mixed greens and the remaining 2 tablespoons porcini oil and season with salt and pepper. Quickly toss mixture well so greens barely wilt. Immediately transfer to plates and serve.

MUSHROOM HASH

Serves 6

This is a great side dish as well as a fantastic topping for pizza or pasta, a stuffing for chicken, or a filling to layer in a lasagna.

Heat 2 tablespoons of the porcini oil in a large sauté pan over medium-high heat until it just begins to smoke. Add ¼ of the mushrooms; do not move them until lightly brown on one side, about 1 minute, then sauté until brown, about 5 minutes. (It is very important that the mushrooms are not crowded, otherwise they will boil in their own juices rather than brown.)

Sprinkle mushrooms with salt, pepper, and ½ tablespoon of the thyme (½ teaspoon if dried). Stir well and add parsley. Mix again and scrape into a bowl. Repeat with remaining mushrooms and oil. Add all the garlic to the last batch, sautéing until light brown. Return all the mushrooms to the pan and mix well. Season to taste with salt and pepper. Cook until heated through, if using immediately, or store, tightly covered in the refrigerator, for up to 2 days.

½ cup porcini olive oil
(page 24)

2 pounds fresh shiitake, domestic, or wild mushrooms, trimmed and quartered

Salt and freshly ground pepper

2 tablespoons chopped fresh thyme or 2 teaspoons dried thyme

2 tablespoons chopped fresh flat-leaf parsley

¼ cup finely chopped garlic

Chef's Notes

If mushrooms are dirty, do not wash them. Clean them by wiping gently with a tea towel or use an old, soft toothbrush.
If you have a large enough sauté pan, you can cook the mushrooms in fewer batches. But you must avoid overcrowding the pan as this prevents browning and flavor development and results in soggy mushrooms.

OVEN-ROASTED VEGETABLES

1 large red onion, sliced
¼-inch thick

2 small zucchini (about
½ pound total), sliced ⅜ inch
thick on the diagonal

1 pound shiitake
or domestic mushrooms,
sliced ⅜ inch thick

1 fennel bulb, sliced ¼ inch
thick, lengthwise

1 red bell pepper, seeded and
cut into ½-inch julienne

¾ cup (about) porcini olive oil
(page 24)

Salt and freshly ground pepper

1 tablespoon finely
chopped garlic

2 teaspoons fennel seed

1 teaspoon red chili pepper
flakes (optional)

2 tablespoons sherry vinegar
or red wine vinegar

2 tablespoons finely chopped
fresh flat-leaf parsley

This is a wonderful, easy way to take advantage of your summer garden—almost every vegetable takes well to roasting and grilling except for delicate ones such as English peas and snap peas. Roasted winter vegetables are equally good and can make a whole supper with a piece of cheese and bread. This dish can be made several hours in advance and left, covered, on a counter to be served at room temperature. It also makes a delicious sandwich filling with Basil-Garlic Mayonnaise (page 33). Some additions or substitutions for the vegetables below include asparagus, beets, leeks, eggplant, and carrots, each cut into bite-size pieces.

Preheat broiler and place rack 5 or more inches below the heat. Place onion, zucchini, mushrooms, fennel, and bell pepper in a large bowl. Pour 3 to 4 tablespoons porcini oil over and toss well to coat. Add more oil if necessary so that all vegetables have a light coating of oil. Season with salt and pepper to taste and toss again.

Spread vegetables in one layer on a baking sheet or in a roasting pan. Place in oven and roast until they begin to brown. Stir vegetables occasionally so they cook evenly and don't burn. Roast until all vegetables are cooked through, about 30 minutes. Lower rack or heat if vegetables cook too quickly.

Heat 2 tablespoons of the porcini oil in a small sauté pan over high heat until hot. Add garlic and sauté until light brown, moving the pan on and off the heat as necessary to regulate temperature. Add fennel seed and red chili pepper flakes, if desired. Let sizzle 5 to 10 seconds. Remove pan from heat and add vinegar. Whisk well, then whisk in another 5 tablespoons porcini oil, parsley, and salt and pepper to taste. Toss roasted vegetables with the dressing and serve.

4 large artichokes
(or 4 marinated artichoke
hearts if short on time)

2 tablespoons fresh lemon juice

½ cup porcini olive oil
(page 24)

6 ounces fresh shiitake
or domestic mushrooms, sliced
¼ inch thick (about 4 cups)

3 cups chicken stock (page 42)
or canned, low-salt
chicken broth

¾–1 pound dried pappardelle
(wide egg pasta)

1 tablespoon finely
chopped garlic

1 tablespoon chopped
fresh thyme or 1 teaspoon
dried thyme

Salt and freshly ground pepper

1 bunch fresh flat-leaf parsley,
finely chopped

¾ cup freshly grated
Parmesan cheese

½ bunch spinach,
well washed and dried

 # MUSHROOM AND ARTICHOKE
PAPPARDELLE

This pasta works well as a one-dish supper. If you are looking for a more substantial dish, simply sauté some chicken or lamb pieces with the mushrooms. In the spring, I like to substitute asparagus for fresh spinach. This is a soupy pasta, terrific for dipping crusty bread.

If using whole artichokes, cut off and discard the top ⅓ of the artichokes and cut off all but 1 inch of the stem. Snap off dark, outer leaves until only the pale, yellow-green leaves remain. With a paring knife, trim the artichokes and their stems of all the dark green parts. Cut in half lengthwise through the heart and remove the fuzzy chokes with a spoon. Slice the hearts lengthwise ⅛ inch thick and put in a bowl of water with the lemon juice.

In a large sauté pan, heat ¼ cup of the porcini oil over high heat until it just begins to smoke. Add mushrooms and sliced, fresh artichoke hearts, if using (marinated artichokes should be added later). Do not move them for about 1 minute or until lightly brown on one side. Then sauté until brown, about 5 minutes. (It is very important that the mushrooms are not crowded; otherwise they will boil in their own juices rather than brown.)

Meanwhile, bring chicken stock to a boil in a saucepan and boil until reduced by ½. Bring a pot of salted water to a boil for the pasta. (If you have used canned stock, do not salt the pasta cooking water!) Cook the pasta until al dente.

Add garlic to mushroom mixture and continue to sauté until garlic turns light brown, about 1 minute. Add thyme and reduced chicken stock. Bring to a boil and season with salt and pepper. If using marinated artichokes, add them now.

To finish, add remaining ¼ cup porcini oil, parsley, and ½ cup of the cheese. Stir well and season with salt and pepper. Stir in spinach just until it wilts and add cooked pasta. Pour onto a platter or divide among hot bowls; sprinkle remaining cheese on top. Serve pronto!

PORK TENDERLOIN WITH
MOLASSES, BACON, AND PORCINI VINAIGRETTE

Serves 4

6 tablespoons porcini olive oil (page 24)

2 pounds pork tenderloin

Salt and freshly ground pepper

½ pound bacon, cut into ¼-inch dice

1 tablespoon finely chopped garlic

1 teaspoon finely chopped fresh rosemary or ½ teaspoon dried rosemary

⅓ cup balsamic vinegar

2 tablespoons dark molasses

1 tablespoon finely chopped fresh flat-leaf parsley

Pork is a very sweet-tasting meat and, if well trimmed, is low in fat. The *agro dolci* (sweet and sour) nature of the vinaigrette is a classic Italian flavor profile that works well with pork, chicken, and veal. Serve the pork with Sautéed Spinach (page 62), leaving out the bacon. Recipe may easily be doubled.

Preheat oven to 400 degrees F. Heat 3 tablespoons of the porcini oil in a heavy, oven-going pan over medium-high heat until hot. Season pork with salt and pepper and brown all over, 3 to 5 minutes. Put in the oven and roast to an internal temperature of 165 degrees F, about 15 minutes.

When pork has cooked, transfer it to a platter and keep warm. Pour cooking juices from pan over meat. Return pan to medium heat and add bacon. Cook until crisp. Drain off and discard all but 2 tablespoons fat from the pan. Add garlic and sauté over medium-high heat until light brown. Add rosemary and stir. Remove pan from heat, add vinegar, and stir up all the brown bits that stick to the bottom of the pan. Add molasses and stir well.

To finish sauce, return pan to heat and stir in meat juices that have accumulated around the meat. Add parsley and remaining 3 tablespoons porcini oil. Keep warm. When ready to serve, slice meat ¼ inch thick and arrange on 4 heated plates. Spoon sauce over meat.

8 CITRUS OLIVE OIL

Some lemon oils made in Tuscany are extraordinary. Whole lemons are ground along with the olives into a paste and then pressed, extracting the lemon flavor with the oil. In this process, the lemon and olive flavors become joined in a way impossible to duplicate in the home kitchen. These oils also tend to be fabulously expensive. Home-made oils emphasize the fresh, juicy character of citrus and are a particular delight for summer cooking.

All the flavors of citrus oils—orange, lemon, lime, tangerine—are essentially interchangeable. If I run out of orange, I just fill out the amount in the recipe with lemon. When using citrus oils, you are adding the flavor but not the acid. Occasionally, you may need to add back some acidity in order to balance the flavors of a dish.

Citrus oils are wonderful to dress greens with effortless panache—no vinegar necessary, just toss with a drizzling of the oil. This is particularly helpful if the dinner is an occasion when the taste of good wines may be harmed by an acidic dressing.

Citrus-flavored olive oils are distinctly different from the concentrated citrus essence oils on the market and cannot be interchanged. These concentrated oils are most appropriate for innumerable baking uses such as for flavoring cake and cookie batters, as well as frozen mousses and baked soufflés, and even for making mixed drinks with or without the addition of spirits.

½ pound green beans, topped and tailed

7 tablespoons honey

¼ cup balsamic vinegar

½ cup citrus olive oil (page 22)

2 teaspoons lemon zest

Salt and freshly ground pepper

4 skinless salmon fillets (5 ounces each)

2 tablespoons extra-virgin olive oil

2 handfuls mixed greens

1 teaspoon fresh lemon juice

Chef's Notes

Cedar planking salmon: Cut a 14-inch length from a 1-inch by 8-inch cedar board. To condition the board before its first use, place it on a cookie sheet and put it on the middle rack in a preheated 450 degree F oven. Roast the plank until it is fragrant and starts to crackle, about 8 minutes. Then remove and wipe with a cloth that has been saturated with olive oil. Place salmon on the board and return it to the oven. Cook until salmon is done, about 10 minutes.
For a dramatic presentation, remove the salmon to a platter and keep warm. Let board cool a little, then arrange beans on the plank. Replace fish on top of beans, garnish with greens, and serve. Board may be washed and reused 6 to 8 times.

ROASTED SALMON WITH GREEN BEANS AND CITRUS VINAIGRETTE

We like this salmon roasted on a hot cedar plank in the old, Native American way. The cedar gives the salmon a sweet smokiness. The preheated board allows the fish to cook evenly from the top and bottom at the same time. Following is a traditional method for roasting salmon in the oven; see Chef's Notes for instructions for roasting on a cedar plank, which is also done in your home oven.

Bring a saucepan of salted water to a boil. Add green beans and cook until tender, 3 to 5 minutes. When done, drain and spread on a baking sheet to cool.

Preheat oven to 450 degrees F. In a small bowl, combine honey and vinegar. If honey is too thick to mix easily, warm it on the stove or in the microwave oven for a few seconds. Slowly whisk in citrus oil to form an emulsion. Add zest and season with salt and pepper to taste. Pour all but 2 to 3 tablespoons into another bowl.

Season salmon on both sides with salt and pepper. Put on a dish and pour about ⅓ of the honey vinaigrette over. Turn several times to make sure salmon is well coated. Heat 1 tablespoon extra-virgin olive oil in a nonstick, oven-going pan over medium-high heat until hot. Add fillets in one layer and immediately place in oven until done, 8 to 10 minutes.

Toss green beans with a little of the remaining vinaigrette and divide among 4 plates. Place salmon on top and brush with more vinaigrette. Garnish with mixed greens moistened with remaining olive oil and lemon juice.

VARIATION WITH LAVENDER OIL: This is a great recipe for lavender olive oil, which goes wonderfully with the tastes of honey, balsamic vinegar, and salmon. Replace citrus olive oil with lavender oil or use half and half.

WARM NEW POTATO SALAD
WITH CHIVES

Serves 4

This is a terrific way to serve small new potatoes, which have the sweet taste of spring. Adding the dressing to still-warm potatoes is a variation of German potato salad. The citrus oil vinaigrette is a pleasant and healthy change from a traditional American, mayonnaise-based potato salad.

In a large saucepan, cover potatoes with cold, salted water and bring to a boil. Lower heat and simmer until tender when pierced with a knife, about 15 minutes.

In a small bowl, mix together vinegar, citrus oil, shallots, and chives. Season with salt and pepper to taste. When potatoes are cooked, drain and let stand until just cool enough to handle.

Slice ¼ inch thick and immediately toss with dressing. Add salt and pepper to taste and toss again.

1 pound small red potatoes

1 tablespoon champagne wine vinegar or white wine vinegar

¼ cup citrus olive oil (page 22)

4 shallots, thinly sliced

2 tablespoons finely chopped fresh chives

Salt and freshly ground pepper

Chef's Notes

By starting the potatoes in cold water, the potatoes will cook more evenly from the inside out.

ROASTED BEET SALAD
WITH CITRUS-TARRAGON DRESSING

Serves 6

Like potatoes, beets taste best roasted in their jackets. They get incredibly sweet and peel easily once roasted. While the beets are delicious served on their own, you may arrange them on a bed of mixed salad greens or arugula to add crunch to the dish.

For a more substantial salad, crumble some goat cheese or blue cheese on top.

Preheat oven to 400 degrees F. Use your hands to coat beets in olive oil, season well with salt and pepper, and place on a baking sheet in the oven. Roast until knife tender, about 1¼ hours. Let stand until cool enough to handle. Peel beets and cut into small wedges. Place in a serving bowl or nonmetallic mixing bowl.

In a small bowl, whisk together lemon juice, tarragon, and citrus oil. Pour over beets and toss well. Season to taste with salt and pepper. Let rest at least 10 minutes to allow beets to soak up flavor. Pour off some of the dressing into another bowl and toss with greens or tomatoes. Divide greens among 4 plates and top with beets.

8 medium beets (about 2 pounds), washed and trimmed to leave on 1 inch of tops and tails

Olive oil, for coating beets

Salt and freshly ground pepper

2 tablespoons fresh lemon juice

2 tablespoons fresh tarragon or 2 teaspoons dried tarragon (see Chef's Notes, page 88)

½ cup citrus olive oil (page 22)

5 cups loosely packed mixed salad greens or arugula or 3 vine-ripened tomatoes, sliced (optional)

1 pound large shrimp
(size 16/20 or larger), shells on

½ cup citrus olive oil
(page 22)

2 tablespoons minced
red onion

1 teaspoon minced garlic

2 tablespoons finely chopped
fresh cilantro

2 tablespoons fresh lemon juice

4 bamboo skewers, soaked,
or metal skewers

Salt and freshly ground pepper

Citrus Aioli (page 74)
(optional)

Chef's Notes

Leaving the shells on the shrimp protects them from drying out during cooking. This method works so well that I use it often when preparing shrimp or prawns for salads, pasta, pizza, and sandwiches. Simply reduce the cooking time if they will later be cooked more, for instance as part of a sauce or pizza topping. Peel shrimp after they come off the grill.

MARINATED GRILLED
SHRIMP COCKTAIL

This is the only recipe in the book that calls for cilantro (the fresh leaves of coriander), not because I don't like the herb. I do, but it is rarely used in Italian cooking. I only used it after I found some old Sicilian recipes that called for cilantro. My guess is that people had coriander seeds from the spice trade and planted some of them.

Cut along the back about ¼ inch deep through the shell of each shrimp to remove the vein. Put shrimp in a shallow, nonaluminum baking dish.

In a small bowl, whisk together citrus oil, onion, garlic, cilantro, and lemon juice. Pour over shrimp, cover, and let marinate, refrigerated, 1 to 4 hours.

Preheat grill or broiler. When ready to cook, thread the shrimp on skewers and discard marinade. Season with salt and pepper to taste and grill or broil, turning once, until just done, 2 to 3 minutes. Shrimp can be served warm or at room temperature. They are delicious on their own or with citrus aioli.

1 small red onion

¼ cup fresh orange juice

Salt and freshly ground pepper

Grated zest of 1 orange

⅓ cup citrus olive oil
(page 22)

4 large vine-ripened tomatoes
(3 to 3½ inches in diameter)

¼ cup chiffonade of fresh basil
(see Chef's Notes)

1 tablespoon basil olive oil
(page 22) (optional)

Chef's Notes

To make a chiffonade, stack several whole basil leaves on top of each other. Roll up lengthwise and cut crosswise into very thin strips.

TOMATO AND
RED ONION SANDWICH

This dish takes advantage of the traditional Mediterranean combination of tomatoes, citrus, and onion. You can serve it again and again throughout tomato season varying it each time with different herbs, different types of tomatoes (even interlayering different colors of tomato), and choosing either lemon, orange, or tangerine citrus oil. The sandwich makes a charming presentation as a first course and a wonderful accompaniment to grilled chicken breasts for a light, summer supper.

Cut onion in half lengthwise, then cut each half in half crosswise. Slice lengthwise into very thin (⅛-inch) pieces. Put onion in a bowl with orange juice and salt and pepper to taste. Let marinate 5 to 10 minutes. In another small bowl, whisk together orange zest and citrus oil.

Cut a small slice off the bottoms of the tomatoes so they will stand upright. Slice tomatoes in thirds, crosswise (do not core them). Lay out slices on a board or platter and season with salt and pepper. Drizzle with zest and citrus oil and top each (excluding tomato tops) with a sprinkling of onion and basil. Reassemble tomatoes and garnish tops with basil. Drizzle each with a little basil oil, if desired.

Part 2

FLAVORED VINEGARS

We have taken vinegar for granted for so long, we have forgotten to wonder what it is and what its characteristics might be. We go to the grocery store and, without thinking, reach out for a bottle of cider vinegar for cooking or a large bottle of distilled vinegar for general household use and pickling.

If we left our habits at home and really looked at the shelves of vinegar in a well-stocked store, they would deliver a lesson in geography and anthropology. Vinegar comes from all over the world. The source materials for the vinegar, ranging from rice to barley, apples, and grapes, can tell us not only about the cuisine of the land of origin but about the staple crops of those countries. The cuisine of every country, it seems, depends in part on vinegar, and each has its own vinegar with particular characteristics: rice vinegar from China and Japan, malt vinegar from England, wine vinegar from France, sherry vinegar from Spain, balsamic vinegar from Italy. And there are variations on these—seasoned rice vinegar; herb, garlic, and fruit-flavored wine vinegar; lemon-flavored distilled vinegar.

All these choices represent only a small showing of the many types of vinegar made throughout history. Indeed, vinegar's history extends as far back as that of civilized man—one of the earliest written records mentioning vinegar dates from about 5000 BC.

All vinegar begins as a liquid containing alcohol. A certain bacterium of the genus *Acetobacter* is ever-present in the air and combines oxygen with alcohol to form acetic acid and water. Thus any liquid with enough sugar to support an alcoholic fermentation (caused by yeast) can become vinegar—and has. Historically, every civilization has made vinegar out of what was most commonly available: Ancient Babylonians made vinegar out of dates, while early Americans made vinegar out of apple cider. Asians used rice; Spanish, French, and Italians based their vinegar on wine.

Vinegar may be made from all sorts of fruits such as apples, pears, peaches, pineapples, grapes, persimmons, and berries; from grains including rice, barley, oats, and corn. The starch in grains must first be converted into sugar so that it can ferment. Vinegar may also be made from sweet syrups such as molasses, honey, and maple syrup as well as from distilled alcohol. Acetic acid gives vinegar its characteristic sour taste while the source material and aging regimens account for the different flavors and aromas of vinegar.

Vinegar making was probably discovered by accident, just as the first wines were. A jug of fresh fruit juice, such as grape juice, might have been left uncovered and unattended. Wild, airborne yeasts clinging to the grape skins or settling out of the air spontaneously began to move the grape juice through primary alcoholic fermentation. Without effective means of preservation, the new wine quickly turned sour, to vinegar, through a secondary fermentation caused by acetobacters. Active acetobacters form a white veil on the surface of the liquid. This veil is called the vinegar mother and a piece of it can be used to quickly start vinegar fermentations. For commercial production, cultivated yeasts are added to the source material (such as grape juice) to start the primary fermentation, and a vinegar mother is added to the new wine to give it a head start toward becoming vinegar and to beat out any other spoilage microorganisms.

The French, in particular, have excelled in vinegar production—with the exception, in my opinion, of the king of all vinegar, traditional balsamic vinegar. It was probably the French who first commercialized the production of vinegar and gave the sour liquid its name, *vin* (wine) and *aigre* (sour). They also developed the process for making high-quality wine vinegar, the Orleans process. (See pages 150–151 for a complete description of making vinegar by this process.) The French city Orléans lent its name to this method of vinegar production, which is still followed by home vinegar makers and commercial producers all over the world who want to make the best-tasting vinegar they can.

While the hows of vinegar making were widely understood and practiced all over the world for thousands of years, the whys were not understood until 1864 when Louis Pasteur demonstrated that acetobacters were responsible for the conversion of alcohol to acetic acid.

More than a century before Pasteur, a Dutch scientist, Hermann Boerhaave, discovered that increased aeration of the alcoholic liquid increased the rate of acetic acid production. To speed acetification and create less expensive vinegar, technologists, using Boerhaave's discovery, sought ways to increase the rate of aeration. In the twentieth century, continuous, commercial converters have been developed. These maintain an ideal warm temperature conducive to the growth of acetobacters and introduce a constant flow of air into the vinegar base. Modern converters can produce vinegar within twenty-four hours. The traditional Orleans process, while producing excellent-tasting vinegar, requires a month or more. Orleans process vinegar is, therefore, relatively expensive.

Of Grains and Degrees: The Strength of Vinegar

In theory, since acetic acid is produced through the action of acetobacters on alcohol in a dilute mixture, the more alcohol, the stronger the vinegar. This is not true in practice: Too high an alcohol content will kill the bacteria, while too low a concentration allows spoilage before turning the liquid to vinegar. Also, the acetic fermentation is not 100 percent efficient; evaporation and other causes will mean a lower conversion than theory would indicate.

Vinegar strength, the amount of acetic acid the liquid contains, is expressed as a percentage or in grains. The percentage is calculated as grams of acetic acid per 100 cubic centimeters. A grain is 0.1 gram of acid per 100 cubic centimeters of vinegar. A 4 percent vinegar could also be labeled as a 40 grain vinegar; a 5 percent vinegar, as a 50 grain vinegar.

Commercial vinegar must provide a consistent level of acetic acid. Government regulations insist that a liquid be 4 percent acetic acid in order to be labeled as vinegar. Commercial vinegar is typically thinned with water to provide a consistent strength. Check the label of any vinegar in your pantry to see how strong it is. American vinegars are usually 5 percent; imported wine vinegar is often 6 percent; rice vinegar is usually 4.3 percent; while the commercial vinegar I buy for my restaurants is 7 percent. If you use vinegar for pickling, I would advise using a commercial vinegar so you can depend on its strength.

The recipes in this book were tested with 6 percent vinegar—except the fruit and savory vinegar recipes. These latter are really fruit and vegetable purées flavored with vinegar. Their acetic strength is much less and they are not a substitute for vinegar but a new ingredient and condiment.

Because people have different sensitivities to acid, it will be necessary to taste the dishes in this book and see if their balance suits your palate. Also make sure to read the label of the vinegar you choose to use: There will not be much appreciable difference between a 4 percent or 5 percent vinegar but there will be between a 4 percent and a 6 percent or 7 percent.

Storing Vinegar

Store vinegar, either purchased or your own homemade vinegar, in nonreactive containers. Glass and ceramic are by far the best materials for containers. Metal and most plastic will react with vinegar over time and spoil both the container and the vinegar. I would not even recommend stainless steel: the high-grade stainless steel necessary for long-term storage is very expensive!

Make sure the lids or stoppers you use are also nonreactive. Save corks from wine bottles to reuse or buy new ones from winemaking supply shops. Glass and ceramic stoppers are very good but are more expensive than cork. Well-stocked cookware and kitchen accessory shops often carry decorative bottles with ceramic stoppers. Another choice is an imported beer that comes in a dark brown, attractively decorated bottle with a ceramic stopper. It is good beer, and the bottle makes a terrific vinegar storage vessel that is good looking enough for a gift.

Beware of metal caps and lids, including canning lids. These will corrode. Some metal caps come lined with a thick paper pad. Make sure it is in place. You can line metal caps with plastic wrap or wax paper but use this only as a stopgap measure, as the vinegar will eventually eat through these as well.

For short-term storage of vinegar-based sauces such as vinaigrette and the fruit and savory vinegars in this book, glass jars with plastic lids saved from other foods work very well.

Vinegar From Around the World

BALSAMIC VINEGAR: An aged wine vinegar made in the style of Modena, Italy. Intensely dark, powerfully aromatic, and tasting both sweet and tart, it is excellent for all sorts of cooking and can be used as a sauce on its own. Prices vary, as do quality and flavor from brand to brand. Choose a brand that is aged six or more years and preferably one from a good Italian producer.

TRADITIONAL BALSAMIC VINEGAR *(aceto balsamico tradizionale)*: A unique wine vinegar, aged a minimum of twelve years in a series of barrels made of various kinds of wood. It is rare, expensive, and an absolute must-have for any serious cook. It is as spectacular as food can get. To be used by the drop.

CHAMPAGNE VINEGAR: Wine vinegar made from champagne stock (fermented champagne grapes before they undergo the second fermentation that gives the wine its bubbles). Since grapes picked for champagne or sparkling wine are picked at lower degrees of ripeness than those for still wines, champagne vinegar should have a delicate, clean acid taste. It may also have a lower acidity than other wine vinegars unless it has been corrected by the producer. Use champagne vinegar for vinaigrettes, and, because of its delicate character, as a base for herb and fruit-flavored vinegar.

CIDER VINEGAR: The traditional, all-American vinegar made from apple cider. It can be used as an all-purpose cooking vinegar, lends its fruitiness well to salad dressings, and can work as a substitute for rice vinegar.

DISTILLED VINEGAR: A crystal-clear vinegar made from dilute distilled alcohol. Good for pickling and a necessity for general household use.

FRUIT VINEGAR: Commercial fruit vinegars are usually made by macerating whole fruit in white wine or champagne vinegar. After the flavor and color has infused the vinegar, the solids are filtered out. The strength varies by brand and is usually 5 percent or 6 percent acetic acid. The vinegars have more or less fruit aroma and flavor, again, depending on the brand. These vinegars are appropriate for vinaigrettes and pan sauces. Fruit vinegars (cider vinegar, see above, is a classic example) made from whole fruit which is crushed, fermented to produce alcohol, then fermented again with acetobacter bacteria to produce acetic acid, may also sometimes be found. These, such as pear vinegar or pineapple vinegar, are well worth trying if you come across them. The fruit vinegars in this book do not fit this description at all and the various types do not substitute for each other easily. Fruit vinegars as described in this book are fruit purées flavored with vanilla and vinegar. They have intense, fresh fruit flavors, a thick texture, and a much lower acetic acid content than most commercial fruit vinegars.

MALT VINEGAR: Made from the fermented mash of malted barley (much like beer). Malt vinegar is the national vinegar of England, where it is the condiment for fish and chips. It is also made in Germany and other countries with a strong beer-making tradition. It is often used for pickling and is an ingredient in Worcestershire sauce.

RICE VINEGAR: Once made from rice and now usually made from rice wine lees. It is usually slightly sweet and mild and has 4.3 percent acidity. Rice vinegar is made in both China and Japan.

SHERRY VINEGAR: Made from sherry wine, this is the traditional vinegar of Spain. It is a medium brown color with the lovely, rich wood and nut scents typical of sherry. Its full body and slightly sweet taste give it a starring role in dressings for substantial salads including meat, poultry, cheese, and/or fruit. Its flavors allow it to blend particularly well with nut oils.

WINE VINEGAR: Made from both red and white wine. Red wine vinegar makes great mustard vinaigrettes and is good for braising meat such as beef and game. White wine vinegar may sometimes be harsh, so look for a high-quality brand. Use white wine vinegar as you would champagne vinegar. Use both red and white wine vinegar for making flavored vinegar; use the red for robust blends of herbs and spices and the white for more delicate herbs.

VINEGAR AND PROTEIN

Vinegar cooks (denatures) protein. In the restaurant, we call it cold cooking. This is the secret of ceviche, the Mexican raw fish salad. The fish sits in a lemon juice mixture until it is cooked. You have to be careful when marinating fish: The marinade should not be strongly acidic and the fish should not marinate long or it will overcook and dry out instead of just absorbing flavor.

The denaturing of protein is also the secret behind perfect poached eggs. Putting vinegar in the poaching water will help the whites hold around the yolks.

Vinegar also helps the cook make perfect emulsified sauces with eggs. When vinegar is added to the mixture, the temperature at which egg protein coagulates rises to 195 degrees F instead of the normal 160 degrees F, allowing for a more stable sauce.

9 FRUIT VINEGAR

Once upon a time, every American housewife made her own vinegar. She began with whatever fruit was ripe and abundant, most frequently apples. If she was very economical, she made vinegar from the fruit parings and cores. She fermented the fruit to make a hard apple cider, then covered the jug with cloth to keep out flies and dust, and waited. If she had an active vinegar mother (the whitish veil composed of acetobacters that grows on the surface of vinegar-in-the-making), or had a piece from a neighbor, she would add it as soon as the cider had finished its alcoholic fermentation. (Having a mother starts the vinegar fermentation more rapidly.) After a few weeks, airborne bacteria would have begun a second fermentation in the jug—from cider to vinegar. The housewife would taste the new vinegar over a period of weeks and months. When it was strong enough to suit her taste, she poured it into bottles and corked them.

My method for making fruit vinegar was born out of a failure, as discoveries often are. I was working with mangoes and meant to purée and freeze them so I would have them on hand when needed. Unfortunately, I felt freezing ruined their flavor. In order to prevent two hundred pounds of fruit from going bad, I preserved it with vinegar, and only then discovered how good it tasted and how much fun I could have with it in the kitchen!

The fruit vinegar technique described here takes only a few minutes and begins with very aromatic, ripe fruit that is not too watery. Just about any fruit you can buy can be turned into a fruit vinegar. My preference is for tropical fruits such as mango, guava, passion fruit, and coconut. Apples, pears, peaches, and strawberries are less intense in flavor because of their high water content. Their flavors are more delicate than the tropical fruits and the vinegar appears to destroy a good deal of the fruit flavor. On the other hand, raspberries and other berries, in particular wild berries that are often starved for water, make fabulous vinegar with this method.

The technique produces a product not immediately recognizable as vinegar. It is more comparable to a flavored fruit purée. The taste—both sweet and lightly tart—and texture of these fruit vinegars give them all sorts of culinary uses you might not ordinarily think of when thinking about vinegar.

○ Use for fruit juice drinks such as freshly squeezed orange juice and fruit vinegar. Experiment with combinations of different juices and vinegar.

○ Make spritzers: pour 1 tablespoon fruit vinegar in a glass, add ice and carbonated water, and stir. The sweet fruitiness makes these spritzers delicious and the vinegar makes them very refreshing.

○ Add an exotic touch to all sorts of salsas. Splash a tablespoon or two of fruit vinegar into your favorite salsa or create new ones such as a carrot salsa and red pepper, chili, cilantro, and fruit vinegar. Black beans and rice is a whole new dish topped with a fruit salsa including banana, avocado, mango, papaya, cilantro, onion, jalapeño, and fruit vinegar.

○ Tropical fruit vinegar tastes wonderful with herbs, especially basil, mint, and rosemary. Blend the vinegar with flavored oils or with freshly chopped herbs and olive oil as dressings for lettuce and vegetable salads.

○ Use fruit vinegars in desserts! They taste great poured straight on vanilla ice cream, or to make a fruit salad, or as a sauce for pound cake.

○ Make a dessert butter sauce by gently melting butter, then whisking in fruit vinegar. Do not overheat or the butter will separate. Thin with heavy cream.

○ Give caramel sauces a whole range of new flavors by adding fruit vinegar. Make your caramel with sugar and water and add cream, if using. Stir in the fruit vinegar last to keep the flavor as fresh and vibrant as possible.

○ CAUTION: When making vinaigrettes with fruit vinegar, use light-tasting oils such as French or Spanish extra-virgin olive oil or regular olive oil, or vegetable oil. The richer, more pronounced flavor of Italian and Californian extra-virgin olive oil is too powerful to complement fruit vinegar.

○ NOTE: Do not subject fruit vinegars to high heat such as grilling over a hot fire. The natural fruit sugars as well as the added sugar make them susceptible to burning.

MAKING FRUIT VINEGAR

The basic components are very simple: a vanilla-scented sugar syrup (see recipe following), fruit, 6 percent champagne vinegar, and salt. The salt brings out the fruit flavor. You can use fresh or frozen fruit to make fruit vinegar. Raspberry, mango, and cranberry are particular favorites. I have never been successful with blueberry. I think its high pectin content does not lend itself well to this method.

Harder fruits such as pears and apples can be cooked in the vanilla syrup until they cook to a loose purée. Then blend with a pinch of salt and strain. The flavor of some fruit—peaches, for instance—intensifies with cooking. These, too, can be cooked in the syrup in order to make a vinegar. Experiment by making small batches with both methods—puréeing and cooking—for other fruits and combinations of fruits.

You will need to taste your vinegar for balance; it is impossible to predict the sweetness of fresh fruit in season and the different brands of frozen fruit. Use the amount of syrup given because it adds body to the mixture. If you want your vinegar to taste more tart than your result with these proportions, add a little more vinegar. If your vinegar is too thick, thin with water.

Try to make your fruit vinegar a day ahead of time. All fruit vinegars seem to go through a flavor shock when first made. The fruit flavor gets stronger the next day.

Fruit vinegar will keep several weeks, refrigerated, but the flavor will be best within the first week. Be sure to store in glass or ceramic containers sealed with nonmetallic lids.

VANILLA-SCENTED SUGAR SYRUP

Makes about 3 ¼ cups

4 cups sugar

1 cup water

2 vanilla beans, minced, or 2 tablespoons pure vanilla extract

Keep this syrup on hand to add to iced tea and other cold drinks or for poaching fruit. It does not need to be refrigerated. The vanilla is minced to make sure all its flavor is extracted into the syrup.

Put the sugar, water, and vanilla beans (if using) in a pot and bring to a boil over high heat. Lower heat to a simmer and cook about 4 minutes. Stir occasionally. Let cool. Purée syrup in a blender until vanilla beans are thoroughly chopped into the syrup. Strain through a fine strainer into a jar. If using vanilla extract instead of beans, add extract after the sugar syrup has cooled and pour into a jar. Seal tightly.

RASPBERRY VINEGAR

Makes about 1 cup

½ pint ripe raspberries

½ cup vanilla–scented sugar syrup (above)

Pinch salt

¼ cup champagne vinegar (6 percent acidity)

This makes an intensely red-garnet-colored vinegar. Use it for duck and chicken as well as asparagus or green beans. Raspberries have a special affinity for nuts, especially hazelnuts. If using fresh fruit, be sure to taste as you go to adjust syrup to the sweetness of the berries. The vinegar should taste of berries and be sweet with the clean, vinegar flavor lingering in the mouth.

Purée berries, sugar syrup, and salt together in a blender. Add vinegar and taste for balance. Add more vinegar and thin with water if necessary. Strain through a fine strainer into a bowl or pitcher. Store in a clean jar or bottle (do not use metal lids or tops) and refrigerate.

VARIATION WITH FROZEN RASPBERRIES: Use one 12-ounce bag frozen, unsweetened raspberries, ¾ cup vanilla-scented sugar syrup, pinch salt, and ½ cup champagne vinegar (6 percent acidity).

Makes about 2 ¼ cups

2 large ripe mangoes, peeled and cut into ½-inch dice (about 1½ cups)

½ cup vanilla-scented sugar syrup (page 103)

Pinch salt

½ cup champagne vinegar (6 percent acidity)

 MANGO VINEGAR

Makes about 2 ½ cups

Mango is probably the most popular fruit vinegar of my vinegar line. It has a wonderful aroma. Pour it over ice cream—and add chopped ginger in syrup or crystallized ginger and perhaps crumbled gingersnaps.

Purée mangoes, sugar syrup, and salt together in a blender. Add vinegar and taste for balance. Add more vinegar and thin with water if necessary. Strain through a fine strainer into a bowl or pitcher. Store in a clean jar or bottle (do not use metal lids or tops) and refrigerate.

---

1 bag (12 ounces) fresh or frozen cranberries

¼ cup vanilla-scented sugar syrup (page 103)

Pinch salt

¾ cup champagne vinegar (6 percent acidity)

CRANBERRY VINEGAR

Makes about 3 cups

Try this vinegar instead of cranberry sauce for your next holiday bird. Cranberries freeze without loss of flavor, so don't let frozen berries stop you from making this vinegar!

Put cranberries, syrup, and salt in a pan and heat over high heat until cranberries begin to pop. Remove from heat, let cool, then purée in a blender. Add vinegar and taste for balance. Add more vinegar and thin with water if necessary. Strain through a fine strainer into a bowl or pitcher. Store in a clean jar or bottle (do not use metal lids or tops) and refrigerate. Keeps several weeks.

MARGAUX'S TROPICAL BARBECUE SAUCE

Makes about 3 cups

My first daughter, Margaux, was born when I lived in Miami, Florida. As you can imagine, as a chef's kid, she was pretty experimental with her eating. One of her favorite foods was BBQ. Being that mango was her favorite fruit, she encouraged me to combine two of her favorite flavors into one dish. The outcome is incredible for adults and kids alike.

Whisk soy sauce, ketchup, garlic, ginger, honey, and vinegar together in a bowl or large jar. Cover tightly with a nonmetallic lid and refrigerate. Use as you would any barbecue sauce. (See Chef's Notes for ideas.) Do not use very high heat with this sauce or it may burn. Keeps several weeks.

¾ cup dark soy sauce

1 cup ketchup

1 tablespoon finely chopped garlic

1 tablespoon finely grated fresh ginger

1 cup honey

½ cup mango vinegar (page 104)

Chef's Notes

Ribs and chicken pieces can be marinated in sauce overnight, drained, then basted with sauce during cooking. For ribs, start them in a preheated 300 degree F oven for 2 hours, rotating bottom ribs to the top twice during cooking. You can also dispense with marinating whole chickens or chicken pieces ahead of time and simply brush them with sauce before cooking, then baste often. For shrimp, dip them in sauce, then grill over medium heat. Once done, sprinkle with finely sliced green onions (green parts only), a tablespoon or so of sesame oil, and, if you want to add some heat, flavored olive oil using dried and/or fresh hot chilies, sweet bell peppers, and peppercorns (see Glossary).

☙ RASPBERRY on RASPBERRY SOUP

Serves 4

4 baskets raspberries
(½ pint each)

⅓ cup grappa or light rum

1 cup heavy cream

1 tablespoon sugar or to taste

1 tablespoon honey or to taste

Pinch salt

2 tablespoons finely chopped
fresh basil

1 teaspoon raspberry vinegar
(page 103)

1 tablespoon toasted pine nuts
(see page 185)

2 tablespoons mascarpone
cheese (optional)

This is a charming soup with a surprisingly sophisticated flavor. The basil and pine nuts add depth and texture to this very pretty, pink soup. Since its success depends entirely on the quality of the fruit used, I would not advise making this soup off season. The berries must be ripe and full of flavor. The sweetness can be adjusted by adding more or less sugar or honey depending on the flavor of the fruit used. Serve the soup as a first course or for a luncheon with a salad.

Reserve several berries for garnish and purée the rest in a food processor or blender. With machine running, add rum and blend well. Add cream, sugar, honey, and salt. Pulse in half the basil. Pour into a bowl, cover, and refrigerate until ready to serve.

Pour the soup into 4 bowls and sprinkle ¼ teaspoon raspberry vinegar onto each. The vinegar will form pretty red droplets on the surface. Garnish with pine nuts, reserved berries, remaining basil, and a dollop of mascarpone, if desired.

VARIATION WITH STRAWBERRIES AND PEACHES: Use 1 pint strawberries and 4 fresh peaches (peeled, pitted, and sliced) instead of the raspberries. Use fresh mint instead of basil.

PASTINA with PROSCIUTTO, GRAPES, and CRANBERRY VINEGAR

Serves 4 to 6

A light sweetness from the binding of mascarpone cheese and the topping of grape relish makes this an unusual pasta. Serve it in small portions as a first course and follow it with something very simple such as a roast chicken. Or serve it as a supper dish with a salad of bitter greens such as baby spinach or arugula.

Bring a large pot of salted water to a boil and add pastina. Stir often to prevent it from sticking to the bottom of the pan and cook until tender, about 15 minutes. Drain, toss with 2 tablespoons olive oil, and reserve.

Put the raisins in a small bowl and add warm water to cover. Let sit 15 minutes to soften and plump. Drain and replace in bowl with shallots, rosemary, 2 tablespoons cranberry vinegar, and grapes. Mix well and set aside.

In a large, deep sauté pan, heat remaining 2 teaspoons oil over medium-high heat until almost smoking. Add garlic and sauté quickly until lightly browned, moving the pan off and on heat to regulate temperature. Add sage, then stock, and bring to a boil. Boil until reduced by ¼. Season to taste with salt and pepper. Add reserved pastina and cook until pastina has absorbed most of the liquid and pan is almost dry. (If you do not have a pan large enough to hold all the pasta, return drained, oiled pasta to pasta pot and pour sauce over it.) Remove from heat and add mascarpone cheese. Stir well until mascarpone has melted and blended in. Add Parmesan and 1 tablespoon parsley. Toss well. Divide among 4 to 6 hot plates and top each with grape relish, prosciutto, and sprinkling of the remaining 1 tablespoon parsley.

1 pound dried pastina pasta
(Acini di Pepe from De Cecco)

4 tablespoons extra-virgin
olive oil

¼ cup raisins

1 teaspoon minced shallot

1 teaspoon minced
fresh rosemary

2–4 tablespoons cranberry
vinegar (page 104)

1 cup halved seedless grapes

1 tablespoon finely
chopped garlic

2 tablespoons minced fresh
sage or 2 teaspoons dried sage

1¼ cups roasted chicken stock
(see page 110) or low-salt,
canned chicken broth

Salt and freshly ground pepper

½ cup mascarpone cheese

½ cup freshly grated
Parmesan cheese

2 tablespoons finely chopped
fresh flat-leaf parsley

1¼ ounces thinly sliced
prosciutto, cut into thin strips

3 tablespoons dark
brown sugar

4 tablespoons granulated sugar

6 tablespoons Muscat grape
juice (about 1 cup grapes,
crushed in blender, strained,
then juice measured)

¾ cup mango vinegar
(page 104)

1¼ teaspoons
ground cinnamon

¼ teaspoon freshly
ground pepper

4 ripe pears, peeled,
halved, and cored (leave stems
on for presentation, if desired)

3 tablespoons unsalted butter

½ cup heavy cream

1–2 tablespoons toasted,
roughly chopped pistachios
(see page 185)

ROASTED PEARS with
CINNAMON-SPICED WHIPPED CREAM

This is a delicious dessert to make when pears are in season. Cooking the fruit in mango vinegar gives an exotic, unexpected flavor, which is at once intense and balanced. The vinegar keeps the syrup from becoming cloyingly sweet. Serve the pears simply with their whipped cream garnish or with frozen yogurt or ice cream. Strew the top with chopped nuts or crushed cookies such as biscotti.

Bring brown sugar, 2 tablespoons granulated sugar, and grape juice to a boil in a small, non-reactive saucepan. Stir to make sure sugar has dissolved. Remove from heat and add vinegar, 1 teaspoon cinnamon, and pepper. Stir again.

Preheat oven to 450 degrees F. Place pears in a nonreactive bowl or shallow dish and pour vinegar mixture over them. Toss to coat well and let marinate a few minutes, while oven pre-heats. Drain pears and reserve syrup.

In a nonreactive, ovenproof sauté pan large enough to hold the pears in one layer, heat butter over medium-high heat until butter begins to brown. Add pears and sear on each side until lightly browned, 1 to 2 minutes per side. Add reserved syrup and toss to coat fruit well. Place in preheated oven and bake until tender, about 15 minutes, basting with pan juices once or twice.

Remove from oven and let cool about 10 minutes in cooking liquid. Remove pears to a plate and bring cooking liquid to a boil over medium-high heat. Cook until reduced by about ¼ to a light syrup consistency. (Recipe may be prepared ahead to here.)

When ready to serve, whip cream in a bowl. When cream begins to foam, add remaining 2 tablespoons granulated sugar by small spoonfuls. When cream forms soft peaks, fold in remaining ¼ teaspoon cinnamon.

Divide pears and cooking syrup among 4 plates and top with cinnamon-spiced whipped cream and chopped nuts.

5 pounds chicken bones

2 tablespoons extra-virgin
olive oil (optional)

1 large onion,
cut into 1-inch chunks

2 carrots,
cut into 1-inch chunks

2 stalks celery,
cut into 1-inch chunks

1 cup dry red wine

10 cups cold water

1 bay leaf

10 peppercorns

5 juniper berries

 # ROASTED CHICKEN STOCK

Makes about 5 cups

I like to use a roasted chicken stock in the winter for its dark color and rich, caramelized flavors. When spring comes again, I switch back to a blond chicken stock for most dishes. Make sure to roast the bones well and to brown the vegetables for maximum flavor. However, use whatever stock (roasted or blond, homemade or canned) you have on hand. Chicken stock is such an important ingredient, its quality will have a huge impact on your cooking. I encourage you to get in the habit of making a batch once a month or seeking out a very good-quality canned broth. It is also possible to convince your favorite restaurant to sell you some of theirs.

Preheat oven to 450 degrees F. Place bones in a roasting pan or baking sheet with sides and place in the oven. Roast until browned all over, about 1 hour. Make sure to stir bones occasionally so they brown evenly.

While bones are roasting, heat olive oil in a stockpot over medium-high heat until almost smoking. (Or use some chicken fat from the roasting bones.) Add onion, carrot, and celery and sauté over medium heat until richly browned, about 15 minutes. Add red wine and stir well, making sure to scrape up any browned bits from the sides and bottom of the pan.

Add bones and cold water and bring to a boil over high heat. Reduce heat to a simmer and add bay leaf, peppercorns, and juniper berries. Skim frequently for the first hour and continue to simmer slowly, uncovered, another 4 hours, skimming occasionally. Strain, cool, and refrigerate. When fat has congealed, lift it off and discard. Cover and refrigerate or freeze.

VARIATION FOR BLOND CHICKEN STOCK: Rinse bones with cold water, then put in a pot and cover with cold water. Let rest 10 minutes, then drain and rinse again. This washes off the blood and allows a clearer stock. Return chicken bones to pot and add water. Bring to a boil, reduce heat, and simmer 30 minutes. Skim foam frequently. Continue to skim until mixture stops foaming. Add onions, carrots, celery, bay leaves, peppercorns, and juniper berries and continue as above.

SPICY TROPICAL FRUIT SALSA

Makes about 3 cups

Serve this easy salsa with shrimp adobo, grilled chicken, Hawaiian fish such as ahi, as the dipping sauce for shrimp cocktail, with broiled lobster, and even as a garnish for raw oysters. In summer, when peaches and nectarines are ripe, use them instead of mangoes or papayas.

Mix together all ingredients in a nonreactive bowl. Cover with a nonmetallic lid such as plastic wrap and refrigerate at least 1 hour before serving. Keeps about 2 days before texture of fruit begins to deteriorate.

1 cup cut-up pineapple (¼-inch cubes)

1 cup cut-up mango (¼-inch cubes)

1 cup cut-up papaya (¼-inch cubes)

2 serrano chilies, roasted, peeled, seeded, and finely minced (see Chef's Notes)

1 teaspoon minced red onion

½ teaspoon finely grated ginger

½ cup mango vinegar (page 104)

Salt and freshly ground pepper

1 tablespoon finely chopped fresh cilantro

1 tablespoon toasted pine nuts (see page 185)

Chef's Notes

Taste a tiny bite of the serrano on bread before adding it to the salsa. Some serranos are very hot; others not very. By tasting first, you can adjust the heat of the salsa to your preference. To roast serranos, place them in a small pan in very hot olive oil. Brown on all sides in the pan, then let cool. Peel off and discard the dark skin and interior seeds.

4 skinless, boneless chicken breast halves

½ cup mango vinegar (page 104)

2 teaspoons finely chopped fresh tarragon or 1 teaspoon dried tarragon

Salt and freshly ground pepper

GRILLED CHICKEN MARINATED IN MANGO VINEGAR AND TARRAGON

Serves 4

Mango vinegar by itself works amazingly well as a marinade for roasted, baked, or grilled poultry. Serve the chicken with jasmine rice and thin green beans with roasted walnuts. For a simple salad, tear the chicken into pieces and toss with baby greens and a vinaigrette of mango vinegar and olive oil. Or make a chicken salad sandwich by adding diced celery and onion to the chicken and binding with mayonnaise mixed with a little mango vinegar for extra flavor.

Prepare grill or preheat broiler. Put chicken in a bowl and pour mango vinegar over it. Add tarragon and turn breasts until well coated.

Oil grill or broiler rack. Season chicken on both sides with salt and pepper and cook over medium heat with no flame. If the fire is too hot, the sugar in the vinegar will burn instead of caramelize. Grill on one side until brown, about 5 minutes. Turn and baste with mango vinegar. Continue to cook until done, about 5 minutes more. Pass more vinegar at table as a sauce.

CRISP PANCETTA AND FRESH FIG SALAD

Serves 4

Even if I do say so myself, these figs are insanely good. Serve them without salad as an hors d'oeuvre at cocktail parties. When figs are out of season, use pears, apples, or Japanese Fuju persimmons, all cut into large pieces. Use the dressing on asparagus, green beans, baby spinach, or chard. Do not use extra-virgin olive oil in the dressing; its flavor will overpower the raspberry flavor.

Preheat oven to 350 degrees F and toast hazelnuts until fragrant and lightly browned, about 10 minutes. Remove and wrap in a kitchen towel. Let rest a few minutes, then vigorously rub the nuts against each other inside the towel and rub off their skins. Roughly chop a few of the nuts to make about 1 tablespoon for garnish and reserve. Place the remaining nuts in a blender or small food processor and process until finely ground. Continue to process until the nuts turn into a paste. You should have about 2 tablespoons paste. With machine running, add ¼ cup vinegar and salt and pepper and process until mixture is smooth. Again, with machine running, add oil slowly so mixture forms an emulsion.

Preheat grill. Wrap each fig half in a slice of pancetta. Stretch pancetta as you work so it sticks tightly to the fruit. The slices will adhere to themselves and not need a skewer. Place figs over a hot grill and cook quickly, turning to cook all sides, until pancetta is crisp but figs remain slightly cool, about 3 minutes.

To serve, toss greens in a bowl with about 2 tablespoons hazelnut dressing. Arrange ¼ of the greens on each of 4 plates. Top with several figs and drizzle remaining dressing over them. Sprinkle plates with reserved nuts and remaining 1 tablespoon raspberry vinegar.

¼ cup hazelnuts

¼ cup plus 1 tablespoon raspberry vinegar (page 103)

Salt and freshly ground pepper

2 tablespoons olive oil or flavored olive oil using lavender (see page 182)

12 fresh figs (ripe but firm), stems removed and halved

1½ ounces pancetta (see page 183), cut into paper-thin slices about 4 inches long

4 cups (about ¼ pound) mixed salad greens such as a mesclun mix

Chef's Notes

If you want to cut down on fat a little, wrap pancetta around the fruit only once instead of twice. In that case, you will need only half the listed weight of pancetta. If you do not have a blender or small food processor, it might be easier to double the amount of hazelnuts and other dressing ingredients. It keeps, refrigerated, at least several weeks.

LAMPONE PAZZO (CRAZY RASPBERRIES)

Serves 6

Serve these berries (pictured on facing page) with biscotti and a dollop of mascarpone cheese or whipped cream. For a pretty presentation, crumble the biscotti into a wine glass and top with the fruit. Lampone pazzo are also delicious on top of vanilla gelato, with panna cotta (literally, cooked cream, an Italian dessert made of cream thickened and stabilized with gelatin), with toasted polenta pound cake, or the powder-puff light cake, sabiosa (page 117). You can also use strawberries, blueberries, or just about any berry you like that is in season.

Combine raspberries, sugar, vinegar, salt, and pepper in a nonreactive bowl and let marinate on the counter 5 to 10 minutes. Cut sabiosa into wedges and place one on each of 6 plates. Pile berries on top and garnish with a dollop of whipped cream or mascarpone.

LAYERED VARIATION: For a festive presentation, use 2 layers of sabiosa. Reserve about 2 tablespoons of fresh berries before mixing them with the vinegar. Place one sabiosa layer on a cake plate. Pile the lampone pazzo on the layer as a filling. Top with second layer and spread top of it with sweetened whipped cream or mascarpone. Garnish with fresh berries.

2 cups fresh raspberries

½ cup superfine sugar

6 tablespoons raspberry vinegar (page 103)

Pinch salt and freshly ground black pepper

One 9-inch or 6 individual sabiosa cakes (page 117)

Sweetened whipped cream or mascarpone cheese for garnish

 MANGO GRANITA

Serves 6

This is probably the simplest recipe in the book and it is packed with flavor. A granita is a sweetened mixture (often fruit juice or espresso) without enrichments such as eggs or cream, frozen until hard in a flat dish or ice cube tray, then scraped with a fork into crystals or flakes and spooned into dessert glasses. Serve this granita as a light dessert after a rich meal with perhaps chocolate-coated biscotti on the side, or, more spectacularly, with a warm chocolate cake! You can have fun with presentation by lining the pan with parchment paper and cutting the granita into shapes such as triangles instead of just spooning it into a glass. The granita may also be made with raspberry purée and raspberry vinegar.

Mix together all ingredients in a bowl. Pour into a shallow pan and place in the freezer until hard. When ready to serve, shave granita into small glass dishes and serve immediately.

4 cups mango purée made from fresh, ripe mangoes, about 5 large mangoes (see Chef's Notes)

¾ cup mango vinegar (page 104)

Pinch salt

Chef's Notes

Make sure the fruit is very ripe and sweet. If sugar needs to be added, the balance and texture will change. If your purée is full of strings, strain before mixing with vinegar.

¾ pound squid
or rock shrimp, cleaned

5 tablespoons flavored olive oil
using dried hot chilies, sweet
bell peppers, and peppercorns
(page 24)

Salt and freshly ground pepper

2 tablespoons extra-virgin
olive oil

2 tablespoons thinly
sliced garlic

2 cups thinly sliced yellow
onion (see Chef's Notes)

1 cup water

1 tablespoon finely chopped
fresh thyme

2 bunches green onions
(white parts only), thinly sliced

1 recipe pizza dough (page 36)

Coarse cornmeal for sprinkling
on baking sheets

8 cups mixed baby salad greens

3 tablespoons mango vinegar
(page 104)

2 tablespoons finely chopped
fresh flat-leaf parsley

GRILLED CALAMARI SALAD PIZZA SANDWICH

Makes 3 large pizza sandwiches; serves 6

It was lunchtime for the restaurant kitchen staff. My sous chef and I wanted pizza but knew we should have some salad. We didn't have time for both. Inspiration hit: We stacked salad on top of a freshly baked pizza, folded it in half, and ate standing up, leaning over the counter. I think we made different versions of pizza sandwiches for our lunch every day that summer. One of my favorite pizza sandwiches is stuffed with roasted garlic Caesar salad.

Preheat grill or broiler. Put squid in a bowl and pour 2 tablespoons pepper oil over it. Toss well and marinate a few minutes while grill is preheating. Season with salt and pepper, then place squid directly on an oiled grill above the coals. Cook squid until just done: It will begin to roll up and the flesh will no longer be translucent, about 3 minutes. Do not overcook or squid will be tough. Let cool and cut bodies and tentacles into ¼-inch-thick pieces. Reserve.

Heat extra-virgin olive oil in a large sauté pan over medium-high heat until almost smoking. Add garlic and sauté, moving pan off and on heat to regulate temperature, until lightly brown. Add yellow onion and lower heat to medium. Season with salt and pepper. Sauté until onion wilts, about 3 minutes. Add water, cover, and steam 5 minutes. Uncover and add thyme. Stir and cook until pan is almost dry. Add green onions and cook until wilted.

Preheat oven to 500 degrees F. Place baking sheets in oven to preheat. Divide pizza dough into 3 portions and shape each into a circle about 10 inches in diameter and about ⅛ inch thick. Remove pans from oven, sprinkle with cornmeal, and transfer pizzas to baking sheets. Brush each pizza with about 1 teaspoon pepper oil. Spread equal amounts of onion mixture on each. Make sure to spread mixture within ½ inch of border all the way around. Place in oven and bake until lightly brown, about 10 minutes. Pizza should be cooked but still flexible.

While pizzas are baking, place squid and salad greens in a bowl and toss with vinegar and remaining 2 tablespoons pepper oil. Season with salt and pepper and add parsley. Toss well. Immediately pile freshly baked pizzas with salad mix, fold pizza in half over the salad, cut in half at a 90-degree angle to the fold, and serve.

Chef's Notes

Cut the onions as you would for French onion soup. First cut the onion in half lengthwise, then slice each half lengthwise into ¼-inch-thick slices.

TORTA SABIOSA
(FLOURLESS POUND CAKE)

This is a traditional Italian cake from the Po River valley, famous for its potatoes and rice. Potato starch is a by-product of potato processing, so it is used frequently in the cuisine of the area. *Sabiosa* means sandlike, and the cake has such a delicate, light texture it seems to melt away in the mouth. The cake may also be made in muffin tins lined with muffin papers. Sabiosa makes a terrific tiramisù (the Italian dessert), or use it instead of a shortcake to make berry shortcakes. This recipe was given to me by Marta Pulini, chef of Mad 61 in New York City, who is a native of Modena and an expert on the foods of the Po River valley.

Put rack in center of oven and preheat oven to 350 degrees F. Prepare 1 round cake pan (9 x 2 inches deep) by buttering and flouring bottom and sides, then lining bottom with baking parchment or waxed paper.

Put butter in the bowl of an electric mixer and beat at medium speed with paddle attachment until light and fluffy, about 5 minutes. Add 1 cup sugar and beat well again until very fluffy. Add egg yolks, one at a time, beating well at medium or medium-high speed, after each. Beat in lemon zest, vanilla, and brandy. Then quickly stir in potato starch and baking powder.

In another bowl, with clean beaters, beat egg whites with remaining 1 tablespoon sugar until soft peaks form. Add ½ of whites to potato starch mixture and gently mix with a wide rubber spatula to lighten batter. Scrape rest of egg whites into batter and fold gently until whites are incorporated. Do not overmix or batter will deflate.

Scrape batter into prepared cake pan and level with the spatula. Bake in the preheated oven 45 minutes or until a cake tester comes out clean. Let cake cool in pan on a rack. Cut around sides and turn out, then peel off paper. Wrap well and refrigerate if not using immediately. The cake does not need icing; simply cut into wedges and serve with lampone pazzo (page 115).

Butter and flour for preparing cake pans

2 sticks (½ pound) unsalted butter at room temperature

1 cup plus 1 tablespoon superfine sugar

2 eggs, separated

2 tablespoons grated lemon zest

½ teaspoon pure vanilla extract

1½ teaspoons brandy or more vanilla extract

1⅓ cups potato starch, sifted after measuring

1½ teaspoons baking powder

Chef's Notes

This cake is so delicate it will go stale rapidly. Make it as close to serving time as possible or make sure to wrap very well and refrigerate. Bring to room temperature before serving. Recipe may be doubled. Use three 9 x 1½-inch round cake pans. (The recipe as is makes a little too much batter for a standard-depth cake pan. This extra batter, when the recipe is doubled, converts to a third layer in standard pans.) Increase potato starch to 2¾ cups.

🌿 PEACH AND BOYSENBERRY COBBLER

Serves 6 to 8

FRUIT MIXTURE

6 large, ripe peaches, peeled, pitted, and cut into ¼-inch slices (about 5 cups)

3 tablespoons quick-cooking tapioca

5 tablespoons granulated sugar

Pinch salt

1½ cups boysenberries or raspberries

2–3 tablespoons mango vinegar (page 104)

PASTRY AND TOPPINGS

2 cups all-purpose flour plus more for dusting work surface

½ teaspoon salt

4 tablespoons firmly packed light or dark brown sugar

2 teaspoons baking powder

¾ stick (6 tablespoons) cold unsalted butter, broken or cut into small pieces

1¾ cups plus 1 tablespoon heavy cream

¼ cup granulated sugar

½ teaspoon pure vanilla extract

Like crisps, a cobbler needs no embellishments because the taste of fresh, ripe fruit is the point of this dessert. Use whatever fruit is in the height of its season. On the cusp of fall, for instance, I mix peaches with quince and will often add red bananas for their richness and subtle tropical flavor. Cut the extra dough into strips, roll up into spirals, and sprinkle or roll in cinnamon sugar as a treat for the kids.

Preheat oven to 350 degrees F. In a large bowl, combine peaches, tapioca, granulated sugar, and salt. Gently mix in berries and 2 tablespoons vinegar. Taste for balance and add more vinegar, if desired. Spoon mixture into an 8 x 8-inch ovenproof baking dish.

Combine flour, salt, 3 tablespoons brown sugar, and baking powder in a mixing bowl. Cut in butter until mixture forms balls the size of large peas. This can be done with the paddle attachment of a stand mixer, with brief pulses of a food processor, or by hand with a pastry blender. Slowly mix in ¾ cup heavy cream until just combined.

Gather dough together into a ball and knead gently on a lightly floured board until it holds together. Roll out until ½ inch thick. Using a 3-inch round or star cutter, cut dough into shapes. Place them on top of peach mixture. Brush pastry with 1 tablespoon cream. Sprinkle with remaining 1 tablespoon brown sugar. Bake in the preheated oven until pastry is golden brown, about 40 minutes. Put cobbler under broiler for a few seconds to brown pastry if necessary.

Beat remaining scant cup cream in a small bowl with a whisk or electric mixer. When it begins to foam, add ¼ cup granulated sugar by small spoonfuls. Beat until it holds soft peaks, then beat in vanilla. Serve with cobbler.

PINEAPPLE UPSIDE-DOWN CAKE

Serves 6

Upside-down cakes are an old-fashioned American dessert. In summer, use ripe peaches and nectarines, even plums. The cake is uncomplicated and not very sweet by itself; the pineapple juices and brown sugar sauce permeate the cake as it bakes. The result is luscious.

Preheat oven to 350 degrees F. Butter and sugar a 9 x 2-inch round baking pan or 6 ramekins (4-inch diameter). Put 1 stick softened butter in the bowl of an electric mixer. Beat on medium to high speed with the paddle attachment until light and fluffy. Add ½ cup superfine sugar and beat very well, until mixture is white and very light and fluffy. Beat in egg yolks, one at a time, beating well after each addition.

Sift together flour, baking powder, and salt. Alternately mix ⅓ cup milk, then ⅓ of flour mixture into butter-egg mixture in 3 portions. Do not overmix. In another bowl, beat egg whites with clean beaters or a balloon whisk. When whites begin to foam, add remaining 1 tablespoon sugar and beat until they hold soft peaks. Scrape ½ the whites into batter and mix gently until blended. Fold in remaining whites carefully, until just blended.

Melt remaining ½ stick butter in a large sauté pan over medium-high heat until hot. Heat until butter begins to turn brown. Remove pan from heat, add vinegar and brown sugar, and mix well. (A sauce whisk is a good tool to use here.) Return to heat to melt sugar, if necessary. Pour a little of the brown sugar sauce in the bottom of the ramekins or baking pan. Cut each pineapple ring into pieces, maintaining the shape of the ring (see Chef's Notes). Add 1 pineapple ring to each ramekin or line the bottom of the large pan.

Drizzle pineapple with remaining brown sugar sauce and sprinkle with nuts. Divide batter among ramekins or pour into baking pan. Level and place in preheated oven. Bake until a tester inserted into the middle comes out clean, about 30 minutes for individual cakes or about 50 minutes for the large cake. Remove from oven and let cool about 10 minutes in the pan. Run a knife around the edges to loosen the cake(s) and invert onto deep dessert plates or a deep platter (otherwise, the sweet syrup may overflow the plate!).

1½ sticks (¾ cup) unsalted butter, at room temperature, plus more for baking pan

½ cup plus 1 tablespoon superfine sugar plus more for dusting baking pan

2 large eggs, separated

1½ cups all-purpose flour

2 teaspoons baking powder

Pinch salt

1 cup milk

¼ cup mango vinegar (page 104)

½ cup packed light or dark brown sugar (see Chef's Notes)

6 fresh pineapple rings, peeled, cored, and cut ½ inch thick

¼ cup toasted, roughly chopped macadamia nuts (see page 185)

Chef's Notes

It does not matter whether you use light or dark brown sugar. It depends on your preference and what you might have in your cabinet. Some people do not care for the stronger molasses flavor of dark brown sugar, others are disappointed in the flavor of light. It makes no difference to the cake. I suggest cutting the pineapple ring into pieces because whole rounds can be hard to cut when baked. The ring shape is decorative but not essential.

10 SAVORY VINEGAR

Making savory vinegars grew naturally out of the same inspiration that created fruit vinegars. For example, I might put a tuft of pea sprout tendrils on top of a rich piece of fish which is itself on a bed of lentils. But how should the pea tendrils be dressed? I want to accent the fish, not weigh it down with another oil-based vinaigrette. Savory vinegars provide a great solution because they are intensely flavored and bright tasting. They allow me—and you—to add a zap of flavor and close to no fat.

Savory vinegars have turned out to be as flexible in cooking as fruit vinegars. They make wonderful sandwich spreads on their own or sauces for vegetables, pasta, meat, and poultry. They can be turned into vinaigrettes usually with the addition of only one equal part of oil instead of the usual ratio of one part vinegar to three parts oil.

Like fruit vinegars, savory vinegars are vinegar-flavored purées as opposed to anyone's mental image of vinegar. The vinegar preserves the vegetables so these savory vinegars will keep, refrigerated, for about a week and reward the effort of making them. For long storage, I would recommend putting them in sterilized bottles and then boiling in a hot water bath for 30 minutes to preserve them (see next page).

Savory vinegars allow a cook to use the garden's bumper crop of produce or to take advantage of supermarket specials. Red peppers, for instance, can be quite inexpensive in season and then go up to three, four, and even five dollars a pound. But if purchased, roasted, peeled, puréed, then turned into a vinegar, the peppers will be available when you need them.

Just about anything that can be roasted and preserved will work as a savory vinegar. For example, roasted red peppers are wonderful as a vinegar—try experimenting with combinations of hot and sweet peppers. Or try a grilled eggplant vinegar, perhaps combining it with roasted garlic or caramelized onion. Shallots and green onion vinegar would also be delicious.

I have given you recipes for three savory vinegars: tomato, roasted garlic, and caramelized onion. You can even vary the flavor of these by adding fresh herbs or using an herb-flavored vinegar instead of plain champagne vinegar.

MAKING SAVORY VINEGAR

Savory vinegars are terrific to have on hand to add an extra punch of flavor to many dishes. They can be used as sauces by themselves and make delicious and unusual vinaigrettes when mixed with equal parts oil. Use Spanish or French extra-virgin olive oil to mix with savory vinegar, not Italian or Californian. These latter oils often have too assertive a flavor to complement savory vinegar. You can also use a good-quality nonvirgin olive oil that is clean and neutral tasting.

If you make larger batches of savory vinegars to give as gifts or to have on hand, you should preserve them in a boiling-water bath. Sterilize bottles, jars, and tops or stoppers by running them through the dishwasher or in a hot water bath. For the latter, place the open containers on a rack or on a folded towel in a large kettle. Add water to cover, bring to a boil, and boil 15 minutes. Keep in the hot water until ready to fill. Follow manufacturer's instructions for lids and stoppers, if available. If not, put in a saucepan of water, bring to a boil, lower heat, and keep hot until needed. If you have purchased new corks, these are usually sterilized by the manufacturer.

To process the filled, closed containers, put a rack or folded tea towel on the bottom of the preserving kettle. Half fill the kettle with hot or boiling water. Place the jars or bottles in the kettle so they do not touch each other. Add more boiling water to cover the containers by about two inches. Bring the water to a rolling boil, cover, and process 30 minutes. Lift the containers out with tongs and let cool on a folded towel or wooden board in a draft-free spot.

# TOMATO VINEGAR

Use this vinegar as a sauce for fried fish, pork, turkey breast, and for pasta salads. It is also good as a dip for grilled oysters and mussels. When making a vinaigrette, combine tomato vinegar with oil in equal parts. In the summer, when tomatoes are really ripe, omit the sun-dried tomatoes altogether. Cut the vine-ripened tomatoes into chunks and cook them down but do not purée them, so the vinegar will have texture.

Heat oil in a small sauté pan over medium-high heat until almost smoking. Add garlic and sauté, moving pan off and on heat to regulate temperature, until light brown. Add tomatoes and ¼ cup water, and bring to a boil. Reduce heat to medium and simmer until thick. Add sun-dried tomatoes and cook until they soften, about 3 minutes. Season with salt and pepper.

Purée tomato mixture in a blender. Add vinegar and thin with remaining water, if necessary. Pulse in basil if using; adjust seasoning with salt, pepper, and vinegar. Pour into a bowl or pitcher, then transfer to a clean, wide-mouthed bottle or jar and cover with a nonmetallic lid. Keeps, refrigerated, about 1 week.

1 tablespoon olive oil

1 teaspoon minced garlic

1 cup peeled, seeded, and chopped vine-ripe tomatoes or good-quality canned plum (Roma) tomatoes

¼–1 cup water

4 ounces sun-dried tomatoes in oil (½ an 8-ounce jar), well drained, or 3 ounces dried tomatoes, rehydrated in water

Salt and freshly ground pepper

½ cup champagne vinegar (6 percent acidity) or herbal vinegar (page 171) flavored with basil

2 tablespoons finely chopped fresh basil (optional)

3 tablespoons extra-virgin
olive oil

3 large onions, finely chopped

Salt and freshly ground pepper

1 cup champagne vinegar
(6 percent acidity)

About ¼ cup water

½ tablespoon finely chopped
fresh thyme (optional)

CARAMELIZED ONION VINEGAR

Makes about 1 ¾ cups

Caramelized onion makes an amazingly rich and deep vinegar which has become my new favorite. It is a great spread for sandwiches such as pot roast with cheese. It is also delicious with pork chops and liver.

Heat olive oil in a large, heavy sauté pan over medium-high heat until almost smoking. Add onions, reduce heat to medium or medium-low, and sauté onions until well caramelized and dark brown, about 45 minutes or as long as you have the patience! Be careful to stir well and to regulate temperature so onions do not burn but caramelize slowly. Season with salt and pepper. You should have about 1 cup caramelized onions.

Transfer onions to a blender and purée with vinegar. Thin with water if necessary so that mixture is the texture of a very thick, smooth sauce. Pulse in thyme, if using. Adjust flavor with salt, pepper, and vinegar. Scrape into a clean, wide-mouthed bottle or jar and cover with a non-metallic lid. Keeps, refrigerated, about a week.

 # ROASTED GARLIC VINEGAR

 *Makes about 1¾ cups*

8 large, whole heads garlic

1 cup extra-virgin olive oil

Salt and freshly ground pepper

1 cup champagne vinegar
(6 percent acidity)

About ¼ cup water

Roasted garlic vinegar, like the other savory vinegars, will never win the ketchup race! It is quite thick, not as thick as mayonnaise, but very like a mayonnaise thinned enough to make it barely pourable. Mix this vinegar with equal parts olive oil for a great dressing for egg and tuna salads.

Preheat oven to 375 degrees F. Cut off the top ½ inch of each garlic head. Peel off outer layers of papery skin and place heads in a shallow baking dish just large enough to hold them in one layer. Pour oil over them and season with salt and pepper. Cover, place in oven, and cook until cloves are soft and begin to push out of their skins, about 1 hour. Uncover and bake until golden brown, about 15 minutes. Let cool, then squeeze the softened cloves from their skins into a bowl and mash. You should have about 1 cup. Strain the cooking oil into a clean bottle and refrigerate to use for all sorts of sautés, for drizzling over meat and poultry, or for salad dressings.

Put the roasted garlic paste into a blender and add vinegar. Blend until smooth and adjust seasoning with salt, pepper, and vinegar. Add water to thin if necessary. Scrape into a clean, wide-mouthed bottle or jar and cover with a nonmetallic lid. Keeps, refrigerated, about a week.

 # PORK SHORT STACK

I created this as a two-ingredient supper dish. While it looks elegant, it is simply sautéed pork with a pan sauce. Serve it with applesauce flavored with fruit vinegar. To vary the flavor, make the sauce one week with roasted garlic vinegar and the next with caramelized onion or tomato vinegar.

Bring stock to a boil in a saucepan and boil until reduced by about ½. Reserve.

Butterfly each piece of meat by making a horizontal cut not quite all the way through and open like the pages of a book. Pound each slice lightly between sheets of waxed paper into thin scaloppini, about ¼ inch thick. Season with salt and pepper and dredge with flour. Heat oil in a large sauté pan over medium-high heat until almost smoking. Add pork (do not crowd the pan). Immediately reduce heat to medium and cook without turning until blood droplets rise to the top surface, about 30 seconds. Turn and cook the second side, about another 30 seconds. Pork should be done at this point. If not, continue to cook until done. Remove to a plate and keep warm.

Add sage to the hot sauté pan, stir, and add reduced stock and vinegar. Stir up any browned bits that cling to the bottom and sides of the pan. Bring to a boil and boil until reduced to a saucelike consistency, about ¾ cup.

Meanwhile, bring a large pot of salted water to a boil. Add asparagus and cook until bright green and tender, about 2 minutes. Drain.

To serve, arrange one piece of pork on each of 4 heated dinner plates. Divide half the asparagus among the plates, arranging it on top of the pork. Top with another slice of pork and the remaining asparagus. Spoon sauce over each and garnish with parsley.

2 cups chicken stock (page 42) or low-salt, canned chicken broth

8 slices pork loin (2 to 3 ounces each and about 2 inches thick)

Salt and freshly ground pepper

Flour for dredging

2 tablespoons extra-virgin olive oil

1 tablespoon finely chopped fresh sage

3 tablespoons roasted garlic vinegar (page 125)

1 small bunch pencil-thin asparagus spears (about ½ pound), cut to about 4 inches long

1 tablespoon finely chopped fresh flat-leaf parsley

4 medium-sized beets

3 tablespoons extra-virgin olive oil

Salt and freshly ground pepper

2 tablespoons caramelized onion vinegar (page 124)

2 cups (about) mixed baby salad greens

2 tablespoons fresh goat cheese

1½ tablespoons raspberry vinegar (page 103)
or mango vinegar (page 104)

CARPACCIO OF BEETS
WITH GOAT CHEESE

Serves 4

I am convinced that Americans' seeming lack of enthusiasm for beets is because they have never tasted a properly cooked one. Who could resist the rich, sweet taste and yielding texture of beets roasted in their jackets? As an added bonus, cooking them in their skins maintains their high nutritive value. I love the flavor of beets with raspberry and mango vinegar. When beets are in season, make a spectacular presentation by combining red, golden, and Ciogga (variegated) beets.

Preheat oven to 400 degrees F. Brush beets with 1 tablespoon olive oil, season with salt and pepper, and place in a baking dish. Bake until beets are very tender, 1 to 2 hours. Remove and let rest until cool enough to handle. Peel and slice very, very thin on a mandoline. Arrange slices, slightly overlapping in a petal pattern, on each of 4 salad plates. Drizzle with 1 tablespoon olive oil and 1 tablespoon onion vinegar. Sprinkle lightly with salt and pepper.

Toss salad greens in a bowl with remaining 1 tablespoon olive oil, remaining 1 tablespoon onion vinegar, and salt and pepper. Arrange a small pile in the middle of the beets. Crumble goat cheese over each salad and drizzle with fruit vinegar.

GRILLED MOZZARELLA
WITH TOMATO VINEGAR

Serves 4

This salad had an almost cultlike following at Tra Vigne for years. The salad eventually came off the menu only to make room for new dishes. It is a great warm salad for early fall though it was so popular we served it year round. Serve it for lunch or supper or as an appetizer at dinner.

Bring a pot of salted water to a boil. Blanch romaine until color is bright green and central rib is just tender enough to bend, about 30 seconds. Remove and immediately plunge romaine into ice water to stop the cooking. Drain and pat dry.

Prepare grill or preheat broiler. Lay romaine leaves out on a counter, rib side down. Cut out the widest part of the central rib by making a triangular cut at the base of each leaf. Place a square of cheese in the middle of each leaf. Season with salt and pepper. Sprinkle each with about 1 tablespoon prosciutto. Make a neat package by folding the leaves around the cheese like an envelope, ending seam side down. Brush each with olive oil.

Spread about 1 tablespoon tomato vinegar in the center of each of 4 salad plates. In a bowl, whisk together remaining 2 tablespoons vinegar and Spanish or French olive oil. Add arugula and toss to lightly dress. Taste and add more vinegar, salt, and pepper, if necessary. Arrange equal portions in a wreath on each plate. Sprinkle greens with Parmesan.

Grill cheese packages over medium heat or put in a preheated broiler about 4 inches from the heat. Cook 2 to 3 minutes and turn over. Cook another 1 to 2 minutes or just until cheese begins to weep. Packages should be soft to the touch and lightly brown. Do not let cheese get too hot or it will toughen as it cools. Set grilled mozzarella in center of plates and serve immediately.

4 very large romaine leaves

8 ounces fresh mozzarella cheese, cut into 4 equal pieces

Salt and freshly ground pepper

1½ ounces prosciutto, diced

1 tablespoon extra-virgin olive oil

6 tablespoons (about) tomato vinegar (page 123)

2 tablespoons Spanish or French extra-virgin olive oil

1 large bunch arugula, watercress, or other crisp, spicy green

2 tablespoons freshly grated Parmesan cheese

¾ pound asparagus, peeled if jumbo sized, cut into 1½-inch pieces

1 pound dried penne pasta

3 tablespoons extra-virgin olive oil

1 tablespoon butter

4 cups thinly sliced fresh shiitake mushrooms

1 tablespoon finely chopped fresh thyme

Salt and freshly ground pepper

2 cups chicken stock (page 42) or low-salt, canned chicken broth

3 tablespoons roasted garlic vinegar (page 125) or more to taste

3 tablespoons finely chopped fresh flat-leaf parsley

½ cup freshly grated Parmesan cheese

2 tablespoons toasted pine nuts (see page 185)

ROASTED GARLIC PENNE WITH ASPARAGUS AND SHIITAKE MUSHROOMS

Serves 4 to 6

This is a hearty-tasting pasta without being at all heavy. It has a good rich taste from the roasted garlic and mushrooms, but the vinegar flavor keeps the palate fresh. My basic rule is cut vegetables the same size as the pasta shape—when that makes sense, as it does here with penne. I also like pasta dishes that are composed of 30 to 40 percent other ingredients. You can substitute green beans for asparagus to take advantage of the changing seasons.

Bring a large pot of salted water to a boil. Add asparagus and cook just until bright green and slightly tender, about 2 minutes. Dip out with a strainer and spread on a baking sheet to cool. Return water to a boil, add pasta, and stir. Cook pasta until al dente and drain.

Meanwhile, heat olive oil in a large, deep sauté pan over medium-high heat until almost smoking. Add butter, then mushrooms in a single layer. Do not move mushrooms until browned on one side, about 1 minute. Then sauté until brown, about 5 minutes. Add thyme, then asparagus, and sauté another 15 to 20 seconds. Season with salt and pepper and add stock. Bring to a boil and cook until reduced by about ⅓. Stir in vinegar.

Add drained pasta to the sauté pan and toss well. (If you do not have a pan large enough to hold all the pasta, return cooked pasta to pasta pot and pour sauce over it.) Taste for seasoning and adjust with more vinegar, if desired, and salt and pepper. Add parsley and ¾ of the cheese. Toss well. Serve sprinkled with pine nuts and remaining cheese.

11 BALSAMIC VINEGAR

My first taste of traditional balsamic vinegar was on a wild strawberry–picking expedition just outside the Italian town of Modena. We put a drop of the almost black, exotic, fragrant, sweet-tart vinegar on the tip of each berry as we picked and ate. This is about as perfect as food can get.

I was visiting Modena, the birthplace and home of aceto balsamico tradizionale, to study how this precious vinegar is made. The balsamic vinegar with which most of us are familiar, selling in specialty stores and supermarkets from $3.99 up, is not traditional balsamic vinegar. It is instead a decent wine vinegar meant to mimic the flavor of the traditional balsamic. These commercial vinegars are made in Modena and throughout Italy and are called aceto balsamico di Modena (the word tradizionale is missing). They are flavored with herbs and caramel and aged in wood. Longer aging usually translates to better taste.

The traditional vinegar may only be made in Modena and neighboring Reggio, both in the heart of Emilia-Romagna, itself the heart of Italy. Italian law protects the quality of this traditional and ancient vinegar. While the term aceto balsamico and a written recipe for the vinegar date only from the eighteenth century, aceto existed long before—the first recorded history of aceto notes that in 1046 Bonifacio di Canossa, the Marquis of Bologna and Modena, gave a barrel of it to Henry III, the Holy Roman Emperor, as a coronation gift.

The regulations direct all facets of vinegar making from the type of grape used for the base wine, and its aging in graduated sets of wood barrels called batterias, to its bottling. To be sold as aceto balsamico tradizionale, the vinegar must be as least twelve years old and is often much older. It also must pass a taste test by the Consortium of Producers of Traditional

Balsamic Vinegar and be bottled only in 100 cc (3.3 ounce) bottles. These little bottles of vinegar are fabulously expensive, but one sniff of an aceto balsamico tradizionale gives explanation enough.

The expense of this dense, dark brown, syrupy vinegar with its seductive, characteristic scents of herbs and woods depends on two factors: the length of time it takes to make—twelve years minimum—and the very large amount of source material needed to produce even a small amount of vinegar. The traditional vinegar differs from all other vinegar in that the grape juice is concentrated before the alcoholic and the vinegar fermentations begin.

Every aceto balsamico producer has his or her cherished variations on the methods prescribed by the government. Traditionally, it is women who are the vinegar makers, but this is not required by law! A batteria of aceto balsamico was often part of a young woman's dowry.

Several grape types are used, but the most common is Trebbiano. The grapes are picked for vinegar making when very ripe and full of sugar. They are crushed to release their juice and then the juice is separated from the pulp, seeds, and skins. The juice is then poured into large copper cauldrons suspended over wood fires. The juice is brought to a boil and boiled until reduced by 30 percent to 50 percent of its original volume. This very sweet juice (also called must) is then transferred to the first barrel of the batteria in the late fall and inoculated with yeast for the alcoholic fermentation and with active vinegar from another barrel in the batteria. The batteria is usually housed in an attic where the temperature fluctuations, from very cold in the winter to quite hot in the summer, play an important part in the creation of aceto balsamico tradizionale.

During the following winter, the cold inhibits both fermentations and allows the solids to precipitate out of suspension and the liquid to clear. Once the warmth of spring reaches the barrels, the cooked juice begins to slow alcoholic fermentation. The vinegar fermentation, encouraged by the heat of spring and summer, goes on simultaneously: as the alcohol forms, it is changed into acetic acid. By the end of summer, both fermentations will be complete and the ensuing cold allows the vinegar to clarify again.

In the spring, this new vinegar will begin its passage through the batteria. Over the years in the attic, the vinegar moves from one barrel to the next, each one smaller than the one before. The largest is probably only 50 liters and the smallest is about 10 liters. By law, there must be at least three sizes of barrels in each batteria. The barrels of a batteria may all be made out of the same type of wood or from several types. The choice of wood is limited to oak, chestnut, ash, mulberry, juniper, locust, and cherry. Each of the various woods adds a new flavor to the vinegar while evaporation claims about 10 percent of the volume each year.

Once a year, from the smallest, oldest barrel, about one liter of vinegar is drawn off for sale or home use. At the end of the required twelve-year aging period, hundreds of liters of fresh grape juice have been reduced to a few liters of intensely flavored, aromatic vinegar that tastes harmoniously sweet and tart at once.

It is only fairly recently that aceto balsamico tradizionale has become available for sale in the United States. Usually, it was reserved to be given as gifts or used by the thimbleful by the family and then only on special occasions.

Many positive health claims are made for this powerful and unique vinegar. The term *balsamico*, as used with *aceto*, implies having restorative powers. It has been considered a cure-all and health tonic for centuries and even to have particular benefits for men. When I questioned a number of the finer producers in Modena about this, however, their answers were always the same: It might be so, but we Modenese have no need of such a thing, and so we would not know!

If you should be so lucky as to acquire a bottle of the real aceto balsamico tradizionale, you may be tempted to just open and sniff it occasionally. It is heady stuff! But do use it: sprinkle it—drop by drop, as the Modenese do—on ripe strawberries where the aromatic properties of the vinegar appear to intensify the strawberryness, or on a freshly grilled, rare steak. It is also delicious drizzled on freshly grilled wild mushrooms, on slivers of Parmesan cheese (an example of the marriage of two compatible local products, Parmesan also being made in that region), on grilled or roasted chicken and game birds. If you use traditional balsamic vinegar for a salad dressing, use just a few drips of the traditional vinegar to correct the flavor of the wine vinegar. You will be amazed at its effect!

You can afford to be much more generous with commercial balsamic vinegar. There are many brands available at many price points. Choose a vinegar that smells pleasantly of a rich blend of herbal and woodsy scents and has a smooth, rich taste both sweet and tart.

2 cups commercial balsamic vinegar (6 percent acidity)

 # BALSAMIC SYRUP

Balsamic syrup is a terrific basic ingredient to keep on hand. Since there is really nothing to do but let the pot boil and the vinegar reduce, it is easy to make while working on other projects in the kitchen. Use inexpensive, commercial balsamic vinegar. Be sure to taste the vinegar to make sure you like its flavor, as reducing it to a syrup will magnify its flavors. Use the syrup as a substitute for the very expensive traditional balsamico; spread a teaspoon of it over a freshly cooked steak with ½ teaspoon coarse salt; sprinkle it on raw or cooked fruit; add a spoonful to sauces. I especially like to use the syrup for broken vinaigrettes: I sprinkle extra-virgin olive oil on a dish, then sprinkle on a little syrup. A pattern of green and dark brown forms and makes a dish such as fresh mozzarella sparkle. A regular vinaigrette might discolor the very white, fresh cheese.

Put the vinegar in a nonreactive saucepan and bring to a boil over medium-high heat. Boil until reduced to a very thick syrup. When it is reduced enough, the bubbles forming on top will be very small. Do not get too close to the pan; the vinegar fumes may make it hard to breathe. Pour the syrup into a small glass jar or bottle, and seal with a nonmetallic cap.

 # BALSAMIC ROASTED ONIONS

Serves 6

I was inspired to create a recipe for these onions by an alfresco meal in Milan. I had been to Peck's and bought a picnic—crusty bread, olives, cippolini onions, and more—then sat, eating in the sun, on the steps of the Duomo. The onions were so spectacular that I took pictures of them and when I got back home, I worked out how to make them. Serve these onions with Braised Short Ribs of Beef (page 167), chicken, Carpaccio of Beets with Goat Cheese (page 128), or as part of an antipasto. Choose the fresh herb for the recipe to complement whatever dish you plan to serve with the onions. Make lots of them; once you taste how delicious they are, you will find many opportunities to serve them. They will keep, refrigerated, for about a week. You can make the recipe with shallots as well. Boil just until tender; shallots will not take as long as the onions.

Bring a large pot of heavily salted water to a boil. Add onions and boil until tender but still firm, about 12 minutes. When you insert a knife in an onion, it should meet just a little resistance in the center. Drain onions and spread on a baking sheet to cool.

Preheat oven to 450 degrees F. Heat olive oil in a nonreactive oven-going sauté pan (just large enough to hold onions in one layer) over medium-high heat until hot. Add onions, season with pepper, and sauté until they are browned and caramelized all over, about 5 minutes. Add thyme and sauté another few seconds. Standing back to avoid being splattered, add vinegar, bring to a boil, and roll onions around in vinegar to coat well. Put in preheated oven until very tender and vinegar has reduced to a glaze, about 10 minutes. Remove onions at least once during cooking and toss well before returning pan to oven. Let onions cool in pan and toss occasionally so vinegar adheres to onions as they cool. Serve at room temperature or while still warm.

Salt and freshly ground pepper

1 pound boiling onions (about 1 inch in diameter), peeled and left whole

2 tablespoons extra-virgin olive oil

1 tablespoon finely chopped fresh thyme, fresh rosemary, or other herb

½ cup balsamic vinegar

⅔ cup heavy cream

¾ cup freshly grated
Parmesan cheese

FALL FRUIT SALAD

3–4 tablespoons
unsalted butter

½ baguette, cut diagonally into
thin slices

Salt and freshly ground pepper

1 bay leaf

1 large crisp apple
(such as pippin
or Granny Smith),
peeled, cored, and cut into
1-inch chunks

2 large ripe pears (such as
d'Anjou), peeled, cored,
and cut into 1-inch chunks

2 Japanese persimmons,
cut into 1-inch chunks

1 small pomegranate
(optional), peeled and
seeds reserved

1 tablespoon traditional
balsamic vinegar or balsamic
syrup (page 136)

ROASTED FALL FRUIT SALAD
WITH PARMESAN GELATO

Serves 4

Serve this fruit salad as a cheese course and it will take care of dessert as well. The roasted fruit makes a great backdrop for the intense flavor of traditional balsamic vinegar. Parmesan gelato sounds exotic but is very simple to make and can be done ahead. The cool temperature and surprising flavor of the gelato make a stunning contrast with the warmth and sweetness of the fruit and croutons. Choose crisp, ripe, flavorful fruits. If pressed for time, you can serve the fruit without cooking. Just sprinkle the vinegar over it. When persimmons are out of season, use more apples and pears. The pomegranate adds color and texture but is not mandatory.

TO MAKE GELATO: Put the cream and Parmesan in the top of a double boiler and place over simmering water. Heat until cheese has thoroughly melted into the milk, about 23 minutes. Whisk occasionally. Strain through a medium-mesh sieve into a small bowl. Do not press on the cheese solids. Discard solids. Cover cheese-cream mixture and refrigerate overnight. The cheese gelato should harden to a spreadable consistency. If it does not, move it to the freezer until firm. Return gelato to refrigerator for a short while before serving to soften slightly.

FOR FALL FRUIT SALAD: Preheat oven to 350 degrees F. Melt 1 to 2 tablespoons butter in a large, ovenproof skillet over medium heat until hot. Add bread and toss to coat well. Season with salt and pepper. Place pan in oven and toast bread until crispy and brown all over, about 15 minutes. Turn pieces occasionally to make sure they brown evenly. Remove, drain on paper towels, and reserve. Croutons may be prepared several hours ahead of time.

Preheat broiler. Heat remaining 2 tablespoons butter in another ovenproof skillet over medium-high heat until hot. Add bay leaf, then apple, pears, persimmons, and salt and pepper to taste. Toss well so all fruit is covered with butter and increase heat to medium high just until pan is hot again. Immediately put pan under preheated broiler and broil until fruit begins to caramelize, about 5 minutes. Check fruit frequently and toss well each time. Fruit should be tender yet a little firm in the center. Pour fruit onto a baking sheet to cool to room temperature. Discard bay leaf.

Arrange a mixture of cooked fruit on each of 4 plates. Sprinkle with pomegranate seeds (if using) and balsamic vinegar or syrup. Add 1 or 2 croutons to each and a scoop of Parmesan gelato.

ROASTED POLENTA WITH MUSHROOMS AND BALSAMIC SAUCE

Serves 6

This dish quickly became a signature dish for Tra Vigne. It was also the single most often requested recipe by our customers! It can be turned into a festive occasion by inviting a few friends over and asking each to bring a part of the recipe. The butter that finishes the sauce may be omitted but it marries the richness of the dish to the sharpness of the vinegar.

Preheat oven to 500 degrees F. Cut prepared polenta into squares or triangles and sprinkle with Parmesan. Place on a lightly buttered baking sheet and roast in the oven until cheese is lightly browned, 6 to 8 minutes. Remove and keep warm.

Heat the balsamic sauce in a nonreactive saucepan over medium heat until hot and whisk in butter by the tablespoonful. Season to taste with pepper. Keep warm.

Heat olive oil in a sauté pan over medium-high heat until almost smoking. Add mushrooms and do not move them until lightly brown on one side, about 1 minute. Add garlic and sauté until mushrooms are brown, about 5 minutes. (It is very important that the mushrooms are not crowded; otherwise they will boil in their own juices rather than brown.) Add thyme and parsley and adjust seasoning with salt and pepper.

To serve, divide sauce among 6 hot plates. Top with roasted polenta, then mushrooms. Serve immediately.

Polenta (page 141)

½ cup (about) freshly grated Parmesan cheese

Balsamic sauce (page 140), without final butter

½ stick (4 tablespoons) unsalted butter

Salt and freshly ground pepper

2 tablespoons extra-virgin olive oil

2 cups sliced domestic or shiitake mushrooms

1 tablespoon finely chopped garlic

1 teaspoon chopped fresh thyme

1 tablespoon finely chopped fresh flat-leaf parsley

2 cups balsamic vinegar

1 shallot, chopped

8 cups roasted chicken stock (page 110) or low-salt, canned chicken broth (see Chef's Notes)

2 bay leaves

6 peppercorns

½ stick (4 tablespoons) unsalted butter (optional)

Salt and freshly ground pepper

Chef's Notes

You can use a brown chicken stock, veal, or rabbit stock, or a combination. I like to use chicken and veal. If using canned broth, do not salt any part of the recipe until final adjustment.

BALSAMIC SAUCE

Makes about 2 cups

Balsamic sauce is a very intense, concentrated sauce that makes simple polenta a dish fit for royalty. It needs strong flavors to match its power, for instance, steak or venison. While balsamic sauce does take time to make, it is not at all complicated and can be refrigerated or frozen. Make a batch and keep it on hand for a really cold night when a bowl of polenta with balsamic sauce will be sure to make you feel warm and well taken care of.

Bring vinegar and shallot to a boil over high heat in a large, heavy nonreactive saucepan. Boil until reduced to a syrup consistency. Add stock, bay leaves, and peppercorns. Bring to a boil again and continue to cook until reduced to about 2 cups or less. The consistency should be very thick, not quite returned to a syrup but bordering it. Let cool slightly, then strain through a fine sieve.

At this point the sauce is ready to be used in the Roasted Polenta with Mushrooms and Balsamic Sauce (page 139), covered and refrigerated or frozen for later use, or finished with butter for immediate use.

To use as a sauce on its own: Heat balsamic reduction over moderate heat until hot and whisk in the butter by spoonfuls. Season with salt and pepper to taste.

 # POLENTA

This is the very best recipe for polenta I have ever used. The ratio of liquid and dry ingredients is three to one. It is unusual in that it calls for equal parts polenta and semolina. The semolina ensures that the cream does not separate out of the mixture. It also allows the dish to cook more quickly and gives it a smoother texture. The polenta should freeze very well if you want to double or triple the recipe. Just be sure to separate layers with waxed paper. Polenta can be served as is; sprinkled with Parmesan and gratinéed; brushed with oil and grilled, toasted, or sautéed; served with tomato sauce; or just with browned butter.

Combine stock, cream, nutmeg, salt, and pepper in a large, heavy pot. Bring liquid to a boil, then add polenta and semolina gradually while stirring with a whisk or spoon. Stir well when adding the semolina as it tends to clump.

Continue to cook over moderate heat while stirring constantly. Polenta is ready when it pulls away from the sides of the pot, about 5 minutes, and takes on a choux paste (cream puff pastry) texture.

Remove from heat and sprinkle in fontina and Parmesan. Let sit a few moments to allow for cheese to soften, then mix in. If cheese gets too hot, the texture will be grainy. Line an 8 x 8-inch baking pan with buttered waxed paper; be sure pan is not warped. Using a flat, metal spatula, spread polenta evenly in prepared pan. Spread polenta to a thickness of approximately ½ inch. Smooth with the spatula.

Cool to room temperature, then cover with waxed paper or parchment and refrigerate. Polenta should be prepared at least 4 hours in advance so it has a chance to set up. Once it has set up, cut into portion sizes such as squares or triangles. Wrap well to freeze or refrigerate for a day before use.

1½ cups roasted chicken stock (page 110) or low-salt, canned chicken broth

1½ cups heavy cream

Pinch freshly grated nutmeg

¾ teaspoon salt

Pinch ground white pepper

½ cup polenta (see page 184)

½ cup semolina (see page 184)

¼ cup freshly grated fontina cheese

¼ cup freshly grated Parmesan cheese

Butter for baking sheet

1 T-bone steak (about 2 pounds and 1½ to 2 inches thick)

Salt and freshly ground pepper

1 tablespoon extra-virgin olive oil or roasted garlic oil (page 21)

2 teaspoons traditional balsamic vinegar or balsamic syrup (page 136)

1 teaspoon dried oregano

Coarse salt

Chef's Notes

It is well worth investing in a cast iron liner for your grill. Cooking on the chrome-plated grill can be frustrating since food seems to stick no matter what. The cast iron insert preheats well, searing food immediately. Also, food does not seem to stick as much. Williams-Sonoma sells the insert for outdoor Weber kettles and makes one for your stove as well.

TRADITIONAL BISTECCA ALLA FIORENTINO

Serves 4

My mother used to make a steak very much like this. She cooked it on the flat top of the wood stove, then sprinkled the meat with vinegar and oregano she had dried herself. She was of the opinion that herbs should fry fast to maintain flavor. She harvested bouquets from the garden and hung them from the ceiling in the closet with the hot water heater. She served a chopped green salad in a wooden bowl, and I would suggest serving the Balsamic Roasted Onions (page 137) as well. This dish is a great example of simple cooking techniques showing off superb ingredients. When I make this at home, friends gnaw the bones clean before my golden retriever, Sage, gets them.

Preheat grill or a griddle or a cast iron frying pan over medium-high heat. Sprinkle steak with salt and pepper on both sides. Sear steak quickly on both sides, then cook just until blood rare, about 5 minutes per side. Remove to a cutting board and sprinkle with oil and vinegar. Crumble oregano over the meat. Let rest 5 minutes, then carve diagonally across the grain into thin slices. Sprinkle with coarse salt and serve with the meat juices from the cutting board.

1 large bunch green or red Swiss chard

2 tablespoons extra-virgin olive oil

1 tablespoon finely chopped garlic

¼ cup balsamic vinegar

1 cup peeled, seeded, and coarsely chopped tomato (1-inch pieces)

1 red bell pepper, roasted, seeded, and cut into 1-inch pieces (see page 184)

1 cup chicken stock (page 42) or low-salt, canned chicken broth

Salt and freshly ground pepper

1 tablespoon finely chopped fresh herb (such as basil, savory, or sage)

2 tablespoons butter

Chef's Notes

If the chard is overgrown and has very large leaves, blanch it first in boiling salted water for 20 seconds. Immediately plunge the greens in ice water to stop the cooking, squeeze out the water, and roughly chop the leaves. The quick blanching removes some of the bitterness of late-season, overgrown chard.

BRODETTO of CHARD and TOMATO

This vegetable stew is a whimsical adaptation of an old idea—making a meal out of what is abundant and at hand. A brodetto is actually a fisherman's stew made of odds and ends of unsold fish and sea-food. To me, a brodetto now has come to mean a dish that takes advantage of abundant seasonal ingredients. Put this vegetable stew over pasta or under fish. When I use it as a pasta sauce, I add basil. If it is to be served with a rich fish, I flavor the stew with savory. I particularly like it as a fall dish to serve with pheasant and then I use sage. To make a colorful dish, I like to use yellow tomatoes and roasted red peppers. Or use red tomatoes and roasted yellow peppers.

Remove tough portions of chard stems by placing leaves flat on a cutting board and making a triangular cut in the base of the leaves. Then stack the leaves and cut them into 1-inch strips. Turn the strips 90 degrees and cut them into 1-inch pieces.

Heat olive oil in a nonreactive sauté pan over medium-high heat until almost smoking. Add garlic and sauté until light brown, about 1 minute, moving pan off and on heat as needed to regulate temperature. With pan off heat so it does not spit too ferociously, add vinegar, tomatoes, and roasted pepper. Return pan to heat and bring to a boil. Add stock, return to a boil, and boil until reduced by about half, or until slightly thickened. Season with salt and pepper to taste, add herb, stir well, and add chard. Cook just until chard has wilted into the sauce. Stir in butter and serve.

PUMPKIN RAVIOLI
WITH PAILLARD OF TURKEY BREAST AND CRANBERRY BROWN BUTTER

Serves 4

This dish was originally created as a Thanksgiving dinner for two as it combines the favorite flavors of the season—pumpkin, turkey, and cranberries—but in a surprising way and without having to roast a whole turkey: The paillard is simply a piece of uncooked turkey breast pounded to an even, ¼-inch thickness. The separate elements of the dish can be enjoyed on their own as well: The turkey alone with the sauce, or the raviolis with the sauce and without the turkey, or the raviolis on their own served with warmed butter and sage.

Bring 4 quarts lightly salted water to a boil in a large pot.

To form the turkey paillards, place turkey portions between sheets of plastic wrap. Pound to an even ¼-inch thickness.

Heat olive oil in a large sauté pan over medium-high heat. Season turkey paillards on both sides with salt and pepper. When oil is very hot, add turkey paillards. Do not crowd the pan. Let brown, about 1 minute, then turn to cook the second side, another 15 seconds. Turkey paillards cook very quickly and will dry out if overcooked. When done, remove to a baking sheet or platter and keep warm. Do not wash sauté pan!

To make the sauce, add butter to sauté pan and place over medium-high heat. At the same time, drop raviolis into the boiling water. When butter turns light brown, add shallots. Stir 10 seconds and add cranberries, molasses, sage, balsamic vinegar, and stock. Simmer until cranberries are soft, about 2 minutes. Season to taste with salt and pepper.

Test raviolis for doneness in about 3 minutes: Pinch edges of dough; it should be tender. Drain. Arrange 2 raviolis per person on hot plates and place a piece of turkey on top. Spoon sauce over them.

4 portions boneless turkey breast (4 ounces each)

2 tablespoons extra-virgin olive oil

Salt and freshly ground pepper

½ stick (4 tablespoons) unsalted butter

8 pumpkin raviolis (recipe follows)

4 shallots, minced

¾ cup fresh cranberries

2 tablespoons dark molasses

2 teaspoons minced fresh sage or 1 teaspoon dried sage

¼ cup balsamic vinegar

½ cup chicken stock (page 42) or low-salt, canned chicken broth

Chef's Notes

The sauce must be put together very quickly, so have all the ingredients premeasured and ready at the side of the stove.

# PUMPKIN RAVIOLI

1 small white or pie pumpkin
(about 2½ pounds)
or Hubbard squash

2 tablespoons dark molasses

Salt and freshly ground pepper

2 tablespoons unsalted butter

2 teaspoons balsamic vinegar

¼ cup mascarpone cheese

2 tablespoons freshly grated
Parmesan cheese

2 teaspoons cinnamon

¼ teaspoon freshly
grated nutmeg

Ravioli dough (facing page)
or ¾-pound sheet pasta
purchased from local Italian
delicatessen

Flour for dusting board

Chef's Notes

While I prefer the flavor oven
roasting gives the pumpkin, you can
microwave the pumpkin as well for
about 30 minutes, depending on
the power of your oven. You will still
need to dry the purée in the oven as
in the recipe.

This filling, with its spiced, savory flavor, can be used to stuff tortellini to serve in a rich, roast chicken broth. Or mix it with mashed sweet or white potatoes to make a gratin topped with buttery bread crumbs seasoned with nutmeg, cinnamon, and telemé cheese. The raviolis can be made ahead and frozen.

Preheat oven to 375 degrees F. Cut pumpkin in half and scrape out seeds. Spread 1 tablespoon molasses in the cavity. Season with salt and pepper. Place cut side down on a roasting pan. Cook in the oven until very soft, about 1 hour. (See Chef's Notes.) Let cool to room temperature and scoop out flesh into the work bowl of a food processor.

Purée pumpkin until smooth, then spread on a baking sheet and return to the 375 degrees F oven to dry, about 10 minutes. The consistency will be like mashed potatoes. Scrape into a large mixing bowl.

Heat the butter in a small saucepan over medium-low heat until it begins to brown. Immediately remove from heat and add remaining 1 tablespoon molasses and all the vinegar. Add to pumpkin with mascarpone, Parmesan, cinnamon, and nutmeg. Season to taste with salt and pepper and mix well. The recipe can be made ahead to this point (makes about 2 cups filling). Cover well and refrigerate 4 hours or up to 2 days.

To fill the raviolis: Lay out a sheet of pasta dough on a lightly floured board. Cut into circles with a 3½-inch pastry cutter. Put 1 tablespoon pumpkin filling in the center of half the rounds using either a pastry bag or a small spoon. Leave a ½-inch border all around the filling. Moisten borders with water and top with remaining rounds of dough. Press all the air out and seal firmly by pressing all around with fingertips. Lay raviolis out to dry on a lightly floured board or baking sheet and lightly flour the tops. Repeat until you run out of dough and/or filling. To cook, boil in lightly salted water until tender, about 3 minutes.

Uncooked, filled raviolis may be used immediately or frozen for 2 months. Lay them out on sheet pans and place in freezer until frozen. Transfer to plastic bag.

RAVIOLI DOUGH

¾ cup semolina
(see page 184)

⅞ cup unbleached all-purpose flour plus more for dusting work surface

2 extra-large eggs

Pinch salt

1½ teaspoons extra-virgin olive oil

This is a good dough for filled pastas because the extra egg makes the dough tender and more pliable. It can be made ahead and frozen. If you do not want to make pasta dough or do not have a pasta machine, sheets of pasta are often available for purchase at your local Italian delicatessen. Recipe may be doubled.

Place all ingredients in work bowl of a food processor and pulse until coarsely combined. If dough is too wet, sprinkle it with more flour and pulse again. Remove the dough to a lightly floured board and form into a ball. Knead dough with the palm of your hand about 1 minute, folding the dough over itself until it comes together into an easily workable mass. Let rest 30 minutes.

Cut dough into several pieces and flatten each lightly, then pass it through the widest setting on your pasta machine. Lightly flour dough, fold it in thirds, and run it through the widest setting again. Repeat 3 more times. Pass dough through successively narrower settings until you can just barely see your fingers through the dough. Be sure there is a light dusting of flour on the dough at all times.

Dough may be used immediately or refrigerated up to 3 days or frozen for 2 months. Let come to room temperature before rolling.

12 CLASSICS: WINE AND CIDER VINEGARS

The first vinegar may, or may not, have been made from wine, but wine gave vinegar its name: from the French *vin* (wine) and *aigre* (sour). While apple cider vinegar may be the most frequently used vinegar of American cooks, wine vinegar is the preferred vinegar of French and Italians. In many recipes, apple cider vinegar may be substituted for wine vinegar of any type. It will add its own fruitiness to the dish. In this chapter's recipes I have indicated where I think cider vinegar would make a positive contribution to the dish. I have devoted a separate chapter to the unique wine vinegar of central Italy, aceto balsamico.

HOW AND WHY WINE TURNS INTO VINEGAR

Good-quality wine vinegar can be expensive, a fact that does not seem to make sense since the wine is no good. That, however, is not the case at all. The wine that forms the base material for wine vinegar gives it all of its nuances of flavor and aroma: The better the wine, the better the vinegar. But just as it would be extravagant to buy great wines to make vinegar, it would be a mistake to think you can make fine— or even passable—vinegar from wine that is disagreeable to taste. Pour it down the sink instead and choose sound wines of clean flavors and good balance. White wines should have good fruity aromas and be dry; red wines should taste smooth and rich and not overly tannic.

In addition, the best vinegar is aged, sometimes many years before sale. Red wine vinegar is often made from wines that have been barrel-aged a year or more. Once the vinegar is made, it also might be barrel-aged before bottling, and given some bottle age before commercial release. If you choose to make vinegar at home, your result will depend, as all cooking does, on the quality of ingredients you use.

A working crock of vinegar could be compared to a sourdough starter. Both are alive—contain organisms that are responsible for the characteristic flavor. These must be kept happy with regular feeding and the right storage conditions. Like sourdough starters, each person's vinegar will have its individual character. Your own vinegar allows you another way to put a personal stamp on your cooking.

I use a good deal of wine vinegar in my cooking and choose a red wine vinegar and a champagne vinegar, both of which are made in France with a 7 percent acetic acid content. I also like to use Spanish sherry vinegar, a distinctive vinegar with a dry, nutty taste. White wines and champagne vinegar are especially good for vinaigrettes for lettuce and vegetable salads, while red wine vinegar suits itself to heartier meat salads and long-cooking dishes such as braises.

My mother, Antoinette, always made the vinegar for our family's use. We liked bigger, stronger-tasting vinegar than was available commercially for the big salads of greens and lettuces from her garden. Because of the vinegar's strong flavor and high acetic acid content, my mother's vinaigrettes were perhaps eight parts oil to one part vinegar. She dressed a salad by coating her hands with dressing and then tossing the salad in a big bowl. Though the proportion of oil was higher, because of the stronger vinegar flavor, she used far less dressing than she would have with the standard proportions of three to one. Commercial vinegars are diluted with water to bring their acetic acid content down to 5 or 6 percent. That water dilutes the vinegar flavor and dilutes your vinaigrette, thus you have to use more dressing to properly coat the greens and to flavor them!

Making vinegar at home is a very simple process. No fancy equipment is necessary. At its most basic, all that is needed is a clean jug, a little vinegar, a piece of clean cloth, and a bottle of sound wine.

The creature responsible for turning wine or any diluted alcoholic liquid into vinegar is a bacterium of the *Acetobacter* genus (high-alcohol liquids—16 percent or so—will not turn into vinegar). These bacteria float freely in the air and will settle without invitation into any open container of wine and go straight to work: They eat alcohol and turn it into acetic acid. Actually, the bacteria oxidize the alcohol molecule by attaching an oxygen molecule to it. Since acetification is a process requiring oxygen, the base wine needs contact with fresh air and the container should be put in an airy location. The working bacteria form a whitish veil on the surface of the liquid.

Temperature, too, is a factor. Acetobacters are not fond of extremes and prefer warm to cool. They will work at temperatures below 70 degrees F but slowly; they will also become less active at temperatures above 90 degrees F. The bacteria are also sensitive to sulfites. Some sulfites are a by-product of the alcoholic fermentation, and more are often added to wine to retard oxidation. Most well-made wines have low sulfite contents; typically, red wines have less sulfite added than whites. Both red and white wines, if bottle-aged, will have lower sulfite contents than when first bottled. Just to be on the safe side, aerate wine before using it for vinegar: Pour it between two pitchers several times and then leave it uncovered overnight.

A greatly simplified Orleans process can be easily adapted for the home cook. There is nothing mystifying or hard about it. You can easily make all the vinegar you use and, if you start with good wine, your results will surpass just about anything you can buy. You will also have the satisfaction of knowing no leftover wine will ever go unused.

HOW TO MAKE WINE VINEGAR AT HOME

The Orleans method, named after the French town that made it famous, produces smooth, elegant wine vinegar. The Orleans process is defined by the design of the converter, the container in which the wine turns into vinegar. It can be a barrel (a wood barrel of oak or chestnut will add a nice flavor to the vinegar) of any convenient size (probably no more than two to four quarts capacity), a specially made crock, or a food-grade plastic jug. It needs a spigot at the bottom for removing new batches of vinegar and a hole at the top for adding new wine. In addition, the container needs one or more holes placed in a horizontal row about two-thirds of the way up the container. If using a barrel, the head (the flat end) of the barrel is the easiest place to cut these. Lay the barrel on its side to mark the place for the holes. The holes should also be covered with fine mesh screening to keep out flies and bugs.

Add 2 cups wine to your vinegar converter. Add 4 cups unpasteurized vinegar. An unpasteurized vinegar is also called an active vinegar because it contains active acetobacters. If you cannot find unpasteurized vinegar, add the same amount of good-quality vinegar and a piece of vinegar mother. The best way to get a vinegar mother is to find someone who makes a vinegar you like and ask for a piece. They will be glad to share. (See Glossary for commercial resources.)

The vinegar protects the wine from attack by undesirable microorganisms, and the vinegar mother gives acetification a jump start. Matching the color of wine and active vinegar or mother is not necessary. If one is red and one is white, your vinegar may be blush-colored but it will still have plenty of flavor.

Add another 2 cups wine at the end of a week and continue to add wine at weekly intervals until the converter is filled to just below the row of air vents.

It is important not to disturb the surface of the liquid in the converter when adding wine. To prevent disturbing the surface, fit the hole at the top of the converter with a funnel with a very long neck that reaches close to the bottom of the container (or the funnel can be attached to a length of glass tubing).

You will notice the presence of acetobacters first as greasy-looking spots on the surface of the liquid. These eventually grow and spread, becoming a gray-white veil. Acetobacters must be in contact with air to do their work. If you splash new wine into the converter, you may cause the veil to sink. It will then no longer be in contact with oxygen and the acetobacters will cease to work.

Over time, the acetobacters multiply and the veil becomes thicker. Eventually, it becomes liver-colored and slightly wrinkled.

If it gets too thick, it will sink of its own weight. To prevent this, Louis Pasteur invented a small raft to float on top of the working vinegar to keep the veil afloat! But it is not necessary to build a raft; another veil will form naturally. Some vinegar makers believe a sunken mother may add off-tastes to the vinegar. When the mother sinks from its own weight, it is probably time to remove and filter the contents of the converter, rinse the converter well, and start over, adding fresh wine and unpasteurized vinegar.

After a month or 6 weeks, begin tasting the vinegar by drawing off a little bit from the spigot. Once your vinegar tastes as strong as you like it, pour the vinegar through a strainer or filter into a bottle. Fill it to the top and cork it. Add the same amount of new wine to the converter. Do not use metal caps for vinegar containers! If that is all you have, line the caps with several layers of plastic wrap. It would be better to have a cork or glass stoppers.

If the vinegar bottle is filled to the top and closed, it will be protected from oxygen and the acetobacters will cease to work. If you like, you can filter the vinegar through moistened and squeezed-dry coffee filters. You can also pasteurize your vinegar to protect it from any further changes. Simply heat it to a minimum of 140 degrees F in an open, nonreactive container. Hold it at 140 degrees F and no higher than 160 degrees F for 20 minutes. Then pour into sterilized bottles and seal with nonmetallic stoppers. Unfortunately, heating vinegar will drive off some of its delicate aromatics. It is best to draw off only as much vinegar as you will use in a month or so.

If your vinegar tastes too strong, do not panic! Add water until you get the balance you want. Testing your homemade vinegar for its exact strength is not necessary. It is simplest to judge by taste alone, perhaps by comparing your vinegar with your favorite brand. But when a vinegar of a certain strength is needed, for instance, for pickling and preserving, use a commercial vinegar of at least 5 percent or 50 grains.

Remember to feed your vinegar converter! Once you start making vinegar, you will learn a new respect for it. It is a living product. To keep the vinegar healthy, you need to add fresh wine about once a month.

 # GRILLED RADICCHIO
WITH ZINFANDEL SAUCE

Years ago, one of my partners in Tra Vigne restaurant came back from a trip raving about a dish like this one. I set to work to figure it out and it took some doing! The trick was giving the radicchio the right flavor and grilling it without it turning black. The secret was a quick poaching in a strong vinegar solution. The radicchio emerges with a bright red color and a slightly pickled flavor while remaining crunchy. It soon became a signature dish, and while it has not been on the menu in quite some time, customers still ask for it.

Bring red wine and shallots to a boil in a large, nonreactive saucepan over high heat. Boil until reduced to about 2 tablespoons. Add chicken and veal stocks, bay leaf, and thyme and continue to boil until reduced to about ½ cup. It should be almost syrupy. Skim occasionally during reduction so final sauce will be clear. Strain and set aside. (Recipe can be made ahead to this point. Cover sauce well and refrigerate up to 3 days or freeze.)

Prepare grill or preheat broiler. Combine the water, vinegar, and 2 teaspoons salt in another large nonreactive saucepan and bring to a boil over high heat. Reduce heat and let simmer. Drop in radicchio and immediately push them under the water or they will darken and turn black. Poach 2 minutes. Try to keep quarters submerged while they cook. Remove radicchio and immediately plunge into ice water to cool. Leave radicchio in the cold water until the vegetable is really cool, 1 to 2 minutes, otherwise the center may oxidize. Drain well and squeeze out water by cupping your hands around each quarter so it holds its shape. Pat dry with paper towel, if necessary.

Brush radicchio with olive oil, sprinkle with salt and pepper, and grill or broil lightly until hot and marked by the grill on all sides, 5 to 10 minutes. Make sure the grill is not too hot or the radicchio will burn before it cooks. Set aside.

Reheat sauce to a gentle simmer and add olive paste and basil. Whisk in butter. Spoon a pool of sauce in the middle of each of 4 hot plates and top with a radicchio quarter. Garnish with parsley.

1 cup dry red wine
(such as zinfandel)

1 medium to large
shallot, minced

1½ cups chicken stock
(page 42) or low-salt,
canned chicken broth

1½ cups veal stock
(page 154)
or more chicken stock

1 bay leaf

1 sprig fresh thyme (optional)

6 cups water

1½ cups white wine vinegar

2 teaspoons salt

1 medium head
radicchio, quartered

Extra-virgin olive oil

Salt and freshly ground pepper

1 teaspoon black olive paste
(see page 183)

5 medium-size fresh
basil leaves

1½ tablespoons cold unsalted
butter, cut into small pieces

1 tablespoon fresh flat-leaf
parsley (optional)

Chef's Notes

Heat stocks in the microwave or on the stove before adding them to the saucepan to reduce in order to speed cooking time.

5 pounds veal bones

2 tablespoons extra-virgin
olive oil (optional)

1 large onion,
cut into 1-inch chunks

2 carrots,
cut into 1-inch chunks

2 stalks celery,
cut into 1-inch chunks

1 cup dry red wine

10 cups cold water

1 bay leaf

10 peppercorns

5 juniper berries

ROASTED VEAL STOCK

Makes about 5 cups

A rich veal stock is terrific to have on hand, especially for winter dishes. Ask the butcher for bones and make the stock when you will be home but not necessarily in the kitchen: You could be working at your computer and have it remind you to check the stock's progress. Roast the bones well and brown the vegetables for maximum flavor. Some custom butcher shops sell stock; you might want to investigate what is available in your neighborhood.

Preheat oven to 450 degrees F. Place bones in a roasting pan or baking sheet with sides and place in the oven. Roast until browned all over, about 1 hour. Make sure to stir bones occasionally so they brown evenly.

While bones are roasting, heat olive oil in a nonreactive stockpot over medium-high heat until almost smoking. (Or use some fat from the roasting bones.) Add onion, carrot, and celery and sauté over medium heat until richly browned, about 15 minutes. Add red wine and stir well, making sure to scrape up any browned bits from the sides and bottom of the pan.

Add bones and cold water and bring to a boil over high heat. Reduce heat to a simmer and add bay leaf, peppercorns, and juniper berries. Skim frequently for the first hour and continue to simmer slowly, uncovered, another 6 hours, skimming occasionally. Strain, cool, cover, and refrigerate. When fat has congealed, lift it off and discard. Cover and refrigerate or freeze.

⅓ cup Arborio rice flour
(see page 181)

⅔ cup semolina (see page 184)

1 cup all-purpose flour

Salt and freshly ground pepper

Chef's Notes

I always dip foods in buttermilk before coating and deep-frying them. I drain the buttermilk by putting the food in a strainer. Then I can sprinkle the coating directly on the food in the strainer and shake to remove excess easily.

ARBORIO RICE FLOUR COATING
FOR DEEP-FRIED FOODS

Makes about 2 cups coating

Use Arborio rice flour coating for fried chicken and fried vegetables such as zucchini and mushrooms. Thinly sliced lemons and whole olives, especially kalamata, are also delicious deep fried.

In a bowl, combine rice flour, semolina, and all-purpose flour. Season to taste with salt and pepper. Mix well. Store in a tightly sealed jar.

CRISPY SEAFOOD
with MUSTARD SEED VINEGAR

This is a good recipe for rock shrimp and other kinds of seafood, such as catfish cut into 1½-inch pieces. Use any leftover sauce as a sandwich spread on its own or mixed with mayonnaise. The sauce is delicious with rich meats such as oxtail, as well. For carefree frying, I recommend investing in an electric deep-fryer. I use only peanut oil for deep-frying, as I prefer its flavor to other possible choices. After making the recipe, fry a small potato or a handful of frozen potatoes to remove the seafood taste from the oil.

FOR THE SAUCE: Place mustard seeds in a small, heavy skillet over medium-high heat. Cook just until seeds begin to jump and pop. Immediately remove from heat and pour seeds into a small bowl to cool.

Combine remaining sauce ingredients in a blender and process until smooth. Add mustard seeds and blend briefly. Pour into a bowl or glass jar with a nonmetallic lid. Reserve until needed. Will keep, tightly covered and refrigerated, almost indefinitely.

FOR THE SHRIMP: Heat oil in a deep-fryer or a heavy, deep saucepan to 375 degrees F. Put shrimp in a nonreactive bowl and pour buttermilk over them. Toss well.

Working in small batches, drain shrimp well in a strainer and sprinkle with Arborio rice flour coating. Shake off excess and deep fry shrimp in small batches until golden brown and cooked through, about 2 minutes. To ensure a crisp result, make sure the oil temperature starts at 350 to 375 degrees F and fry in small batches. Do not poke shrimp as they cook or you will tear the coating. As each batch is cooked, drain on paper towels and season with salt and pepper. Keep warm.

Pour 1 to 2 tablespoons mustard seed vinegar on each of 6 warm plates or pour onto a platter. Divide shrimp among plates and serve immediately.

MUSTARD SEED VINEGAR SAUCE

1½ teaspoons black mustard seeds

2 tablespoons Dijon mustard

½ cup hot sweet mustard (see Chef's Notes)

¼ cup champagne vinegar or apple cider vinegar

1 teaspoon minced shallots

¼ teaspoon salt

Pinch freshly ground pepper

DEEP-FRIED SHRIMP

4 cups peanut oil for deep-frying

1 pound rock shrimp

1 cup buttermilk

1 cup Arborio Rice Flour Coating (facing page)

Salt and freshly ground pepper

Chef's Notes

The flavor of hot sweet mustards varies from brand to brand. I use Napa Valley Mustard Company Hot Sweet Mustard. If you use a different mustard, taste the sauce for balance. It should taste slightly sweet, a little spicy, and a bit tart: the sweetness underscores the sweetness of the seafood, the spice perks up the taste buds, and the crispness of the vinegar cuts the heaviness of deep frying.

2 tablespoons unsalted butter

1 bay leaf

½ tablespoon balsamic vinegar

½ tablespoon freshly squeezed lemon juice

1 dozen fresh figs, halved; or 2 ripe pears, cored and sliced ¼ inch thick; or 2 cups fresh grapes

Salt and freshly ground pepper

 # WARM SPINACH SALAD WITH OVEN-DRIED FRUIT

Serves 4

Hearty greens, such as spinach, kale, and chard, are often simply cooked and served with vinegar. This spinach salad derives from that traditional idea. The bacon adds depth of flavor; however, to keep the cholesterol count down, I suggest making the dressing with extra-virgin olive oil. The purpose of the oven-dried fruit technique is to intensify flavor. The technique can be applied to many fruits including pears, apples, grapes, persimmons, figs, and tomatoes. Experiment with other fruits as well. The low oven temperature is important so that the fruit dries but does not really cook. The more moist the fruit, the longer the drying will take. A convection oven works particularly well but the method works in all ovens that can maintain an even, low temperature.

FOR THE OVEN-DRIED FRUIT: Preheat oven to 200 degrees F. Melt butter with bay leaf in an ovenproof, nonreactive sauté pan over medium heat until butter starts to turn brown. Remove pan from heat and let cool a few seconds. Add vinegar and lemon juice. (Stand back; the vinegar hitting the hot butter may make the pan spit at you!) Add fruit, season with salt and pepper, and toss well to coat. (If using pears or apples, spread slices on a nonreactive baking sheet after tossing with butter mixture in sauté pan.) Place pan in oven and let fruit dry until edges start to dehydrate and wrinkle, and the fruit is still moist and not too chewy, 2 to 3 hours. Check progress and turn fruit occasionally so it dries evenly. You want fruit to dry, not cook. Remove and let cool. Discard bay leaf.

FOR THE SALAD: Preheat oven to 350 degrees F. In a small, ovenproof sauté pan, melt butter over medium heat. Add bread and toss to coat well. Season with salt and pepper. Place pan in oven and toast bread until crispy and brown, about 15 minutes. Turn pieces to make sure they brown evenly. Remove, drain on paper towels, and reserve.

Heat a large sauté pan over medium-high heat. Add bacon and cook until ¾ done. It should be crispy but still moist. Remove bacon and drain on paper towels. Drain off fat and discard.

Return pan to medium-high heat and add olive oil. Heat until almost smoking, then add garlic. Sauté quickly, moving pan off and on heat to regulate temperature, until garlic is lightly toasted, about 1 minute. Add sage and stir. Add vinegar and bring just to a boil. Remove from heat, add bacon, and stir. Adjust seasoning with salt and pepper.

Arrange spinach in a salad bowl. Tear larger leaves into pieces if necessary. Add oven-dried fruit and croutons. Pour dressing over while still warm and mix well.

1 tablespoon unsalted butter

8 pieces good crusty bread,
crusts removed,
and cut into ¾-x-2-inch strips

Salt and freshly ground pepper

¼ pound bacon,
cut into ½-inch pieces

3 tablespoons extra-virgin
olive oil or flavored olive oil
such as porcini (page 24) or
roasted garlic (page 21)

2 tablespoons finely
sliced garlic

½ tablespoon finely chopped
sage or ½ teaspoon dried sage

¼ cup red wine vinegar
or apple cider vinegar

½ pound baby spinach

Chef's Notes

If you have a rack with closely spaced wires, you may place the fruit on it with a pan below to catch drips. Increased air circulation will allow the fruit to dry more quickly. A convection oven would also allow faster drying.

Large handful soaked wood chips for smoking in barbecue (see Chef's Notes)

3 tablespoons extra-virgin olive oil

1 tablespoon finely chopped garlic

1 large onion, cut into ¼-inch dice

1 carrot, cut into ¼-inch dice

1 stalk celery, cut into ¼-inch dice

1 tablespoon finely chopped fresh thyme

1 bay leaf

4 cups chicken stock (page 42) or low-salt, canned chicken broth

½ pound dried green lentils

Salt and freshly ground pepper

1 cup shelled, raw shelling peas and/or beans such as English green peas, limas, or favas (about 1 pound in shells)

2 tablespoons or more sherry vinegar

2 tablespoons or more finely chopped fresh flat-leaf parsley

SMOKED LENTIL AND SHELLING BEAN STEW

This is just an incredibly good dish. Smoking gives the lentils a very meaty character, almost as if the all-vegetable stew includes sausages. I came up with the idea of smoking lentils when I was composing a vegetarian menu to match a set of wonderful red wines. When we make this dish at Tra Vigne, we use three kinds of lentils: Moroccan, Turkish, and French. Because they have different cooking times, we cook them separately, then mix them together before smoking them. If you have time, you might want to experiment with different lentils as well. Though it sounds time-consuming to smoke tiny things like lentils, it takes just fifteen minutes in a covered grill. I like to serve the stew by itself, or as a bed for roasted cod, or with sausage. I even thin it with oil and vinegar to use as a warm vinaigrette for Belgian endive and asparagus.

Prepare grill and soak wood chips for smoking. Heat 2 tablespoons olive oil in a sauce pan over medium-high heat until almost smoking. Add garlic and sauté until light brown, moving the pan off and on the heat to regulate temperature. Add onion, carrot, and celery and sauté about 2 minutes. Lower heat to medium and cook until vegetables are soft, about 10 minutes. Add thyme and bay leaf. Add 2½ cups stock, bring to a boil and add lentils, 1 teaspoon salt, and ¼ teaspoon pepper. Lower heat to a simmer, cover, and cook until lentils are about half done, about 15 minutes. Add more stock if necessary.

Spread lentils and their cooking liquid on a heavy baking sheet with sides. Add soaked chips to coals, put uncovered baking sheet on grill, and cover barbecue with its lid. Smoke about 15 minutes. (Recipe can be done a day ahead to this point.) Pour lentils into a bowl, cover, and refrigerate. (The smoked flavor will intensify and distribute evenly through the lentils if allowed to rest overnight. However, the result will also be delicious if you proceed straight ahead.)

Put lentils in a deep saucepan and add shelling peas or beans. Add another ¾ to 1 cup stock. The texture should be stewlike. Bring to a boil and simmer until vegetables are tender, about 5 minutes. Remove and discard bay leaf. Add 2 tablespoons vinegar and remaining 1 tablespoon oil, and taste for seasoning. Adjust with salt, pepper, and more vinegar if necessary. Sprinkle parsley over each serving.

Chef's Notes

You may use frozen peas and limas instead of fresh, just be careful not to overcook them. Other substitutions would include peeled and chopped tomatoes, roasted red peppers, or even peeled and chopped apples or pears. If you like a strong smoked flavor, cook the lentils a little less on the stove and smoke them longer. If you prefer just a hint of smoked flavor, cook lentils longer on the stove and cut smoking time. The wood used for smoking adds its own flavor. Oak is always good, as is apple. But in a pinch, I have used soaked kindling. Whatever wood you use must not be treated with chemicals.

PICKLED SHRIMP
AND VEGETABLE SALAD

Serves 4 to 6

Use your imagination when choosing vegetables for this dish. Some suggestions include carrots, garlic cloves, mushrooms, red onions, fennel, and bell peppers. Remember to look for contrast in flavor, color, and texture and utilize produce that is in season. The salad should be lightly dressed and the dressing taste only lightly acidic because the vegetables will already taste bright from the pickling. Feel free to double the salad ingredients and cook them in the same amount of pickling liquid specified here. In that case, you may want to cook in batches to make sure the liquid is hot enough to cook all the ingredients evenly.

In a large nonreactive stockpot, put the water, vinegar, white wine, kosher salt, peppercorns, pickling spice, lemon, bay leaf, and finely chopped onion, carrot, and celery. Bring to a boil over high heat, reduce to a simmer, and cook 3 minutes. Strain, discard vegetables and spices, and return liquid to a boil.

Cut all the vegetables to be pickled into ½-inch pieces. Slice mushrooms about ¼ inch thick. Cook each vegetable separately in the simmering pickling liquid until tender but still firm. None will take longer than about 3 minutes. Remove and spread out on a baking sheet to cool.

Bring pickling liquid to a boil again and add shrimp. Immediately remove pot from heat and let shrimp sit until done, about 3 minutes (see Chef's Notes). Remove and let cool, then peel and devein. Butterfly shrimp by cutting almost all the way through their backs up to half their length. Discard pickling liquid.

(continued on next page)

4 cups water

1 cup champagne vinegar or apple cider vinegar

1½ cups dry white wine

2 tablespoons kosher salt

½ tablespoon white peppercorns

2 tablespoons pickling spice

1 lemon, cut in half

1 bay leaf

½ cup finely chopped onion

¼ cup finely chopped carrot

¼ cup finely chopped celery

4 cups mixed vegetables for pickling (such as carrots, red onion, fennel, sweet peppers, celery, celery root, and fresh or dried and rehydrated domestic or wild mushrooms such as shiitake)

1 pound large shrimp (size 16/20 or larger), shell on

GARLIC VINAIGRETTE

¼ cup roasted garlic vinegar
(page 125)

¼ cup regular olive oil or
Spanish or French extra-virgin
olive oil

1 tablespoon minced shallots

Salt and freshly ground pepper

2 tablespoons finely chopped
fresh flat-leaf parsley

4–6 large leaves Bibb
or butter lettuce

Chef's Notes

Shrimp toughens easily when cooked
at too high a heat. This technique
of dropping them in boiling liquid
and then immediately removing the
pot from the heat results in very
tender shrimp.

In a small bowl, whisk together the roasted garlic vinegar, olive oil, shallots, and salt and pepper to taste. Put the pickled vegetables, shrimp, and parsley in another bowl and coat lightly with dressing. To serve, place a lettuce leaf in the center of each plate. Arrange shrimp in a circle around the lettuce leaf, standing them on their spread-out butterflied tails. Mound vegetables in the center.

VARIATION WITH ROASTED GARLIC OIL: You can make a dressing with ½ cup roasted garlic oil and 2 tablespoons champagne vinegar or apple cider vinegar instead of the roasted garlic vinegar and olive oil. If you have neither roasted garlic vinegar nor oil, use the same quantity of Spanish or French extra-virgin olive oil (these have a lighter taste than oils from Italy and California). Add champagne vinegar or apple cider vinegar, shallots, salt, pepper, and a tablespoon or two of roasted garlic paste. If you only have fresh garlic, use a tablespoon but cook first in olive oil until light brown.

PASTA WITH BRAISED RABBIT SAUCE

Serves 4 to 6

Rabbit is very high in protein and low in fat. It does not taste at all gamey but has a mild flavor. Neither does it taste like chicken—but like rabbit! It is also very simple to cook—lending itself to frying, roasting, baking, braising, and grilling. If all you can find is frozen rabbit, cook it anyway. You will have great results. Make two or three times the amount of rabbit sauce you will need and freeze it. Increasing the amounts only marginally increases the amount of time it takes to prepare and you can reap the benefits thereafter on the spur of the moment!

Place rabbit in a shallow, flat nonreactive dish and season well with salt and pepper. Mix together 2 tablespoons vinegar and 1 teaspoon thyme. Pour over rabbit, coating well. Cover loosely and let marinate 15 to 20 minutes.

Heat 3 tablespoons olive oil in a nonreactive deep saucepan or Dutch oven over medium-high heat until almost smoking. Add rabbit and brown on all sides. Remove to a plate. Add 1 teaspoon garlic, and onion, carrot, and celery to the pot and sauté over medium to medium-high heat until vegetables are browned, about 10 minutes. Make sure to scrape up the browned bits from the bottom and sides of the pan. Add bay leaves, remaining 4 tablespoons vinegar, and red wine. Bring to a boil and boil until reduced by half. Add stock, return to a boil, add rabbit, and simmer, covered, until rabbit is just tender, about 12 minutes.

Remove rabbit and let cool. Return cooking liquid to a boil and boil until reduced by two-thirds. Strain, skim, and reserve. Cut rabbit meat off bones into ½-inch pieces and reserve.

Place a sauté pan over medium-high heat and add pancetta. Cook until crispy and rendered of fat. Remove and drain pancetta on paper towels. Discard fat. Add remaining 2 tablespoons olive oil and 2 tablespoons butter to sauté pan and return to medium-high heat. Add mushrooms in one layer and do not move them for 1 minute. Then sauté until brown, about 4 minutes. Add remaining 1 tablespoon garlic and sauté until light brown. Add remaining 2 teaspoons thyme and reserved pancetta. Add reserved rabbit cooking liquid and cook until reduced to a thick sauce consistency. Add rabbit meat and heat through. (Recipe can be made ahead to this point and frozen.) When ready to serve, reheat sauce and stir in remaining 2 tablespoons butter, if desired.

Bring a large pot of salted water to a boil, add pasta, and cook until al dente. Drain into a large, warmed serving bowl and add rabbit sauce, parsley, and Parmesan. Toss well and serve.

1 frying rabbit
(about 2½ pounds), split in half
down the back

Salt and freshly ground pepper

6 tablespoons red wine vinegar

1 tablespoon finely chopped
fresh thyme

5 tablespoons extra-virgin
olive oil

1 tablespoon plus 1 teaspoon
finely chopped garlic

1 large onion, finely chopped

1 carrot, finely chopped

1 stalk celery, finely chopped

2 bay leaves

2 cups dry red wine

4 cups chicken stock
(page 42) or low-salt,
canned chicken broth

3 ounces pancetta, diced
(see page 183)

¼–½ stick (2 to 4 tablespoons)
unsalted butter

¼ pound fresh shiitake
or other wild mushrooms

1 pound dried pasta
(such as penne or rigatoncini)

2 tablespoons finely chopped
fresh flat-leaf parsley

½ cup freshly grated
Parmesan cheese

SPICED, ROASTED CHICKEN
WITH ARUGULA

Serves 4; makes about 1 cup
spice mixture

SPICE MIXTURE

¼ cup fennel seed

1 tablespoon coriander seeds

1 tablespoon New Mexican
red pepper flakes (see page 183)

¼ cup (1 ounce) pure
California chili powder
(see page 182)

1 tablespoon
white peppercorns

1 tablespoon black peppercorns

2 tablespoons kosher salt

2 tablespoons
ground cinnamon

Centuries ago the spice route extended from the Far East through Africa and up through Sicily to Milan and then to Europe. Many of the spices in this recipe were used as legal tender along the route. To use them all so generously in ancient times would have been a lavish display of wealth. The spice mixture gives a complex, spicy-hot flavor to the chicken. Make enough of the mixture to keep in a jar by the stove and add it to all sorts of dishes for an extra amp of flavor. The spice mixture is also good rubbed into all types of poultry and rich fish, such as tuna, salmon, mackerel, and sardines. Grinding fresh or toasted whole spices makes a big difference in your cooking. If you have enough time, make the basic brine on page 167 and brine the chicken up to an hour before coating it with spices. The chicken may be roasted, without added fat.

FOR THE SPICE MIXTURE: Put fennel and coriander seeds in a small dry pan and place over medium-high heat just until they begin to brown and smoke, about 1 minute. Immediately pour seeds into a bowl to cool.

Pour seeds, red pepper flakes, chili powder, and white and black peppercorns into a blender and grind until fine. Add kosher salt and cinnamon and blend again. You may have to remove the blender jar from the base and shake it occasionally to get the spices to grind evenly. If the blades stick, pour the spices through a sieve and put the larger pieces back in the blender. A coffee grinder used only for spices is particularly well suited to this job.

(continued on next page)

CHICKEN

1 whole chicken
(about 3 pounds), cut in half
down the back

3 tablespoons unsalted butter

3 cups chicken stock
(page 42) or low-salt,
canned chicken broth

2 tablespoons sherry vinegar

2 tablespoons finely chopped,
fresh flat-leaf parsley

1 large bunch arugula

FOR THE CHICKEN: Lay chicken, skin side up, in a nonreactive pan and rub about 3 tablespoons spice mixture all over chicken. (If you have brined the chicken, drain it and pat dry with paper towels.) You should have an even coating on all sides. Cover and refrigerate 1 hour or longer (but no more than 24 hours). The moisture in the chicken will turn the spice coating into a crust.

Preheat oven to 450 degrees F. Melt butter in a pan large enough to hold the chicken in one layer over medium heat. Arrange chicken in pan and place in oven. Roast until chicken is done, about 20 minutes. Baste several times with the butter in the pan.

While chicken is roasting, bring chicken stock to a boil in a saucepan and boil until reduced by half. When chicken is done, remove to a platter and keep warm. Pour off half the fat in the roasting pan and add reduced stock. Stir well to scrape up all the browned bits on bottom of pan. Place over medium-high heat and reduce almost to a syrup, about 5 minutes. Whisk in vinegar and parsley, and taste for seasoning. Set aside.

Carve chicken into serving pieces and divide among 4 plates. Spoon some of the pan sauce over each serving. Scrape remaining sauce in the pan over arugula in a bowl and toss well. Divide arugula among the plates and serve immediately.

BRAISED SHORT RIBS OF BEEF

Serves 4

This is a wonderful, hearty winter dish. It takes some time to prepare but can be done ahead (and even frozen) and reheated. Serve the short ribs with a soft polenta flavored with roasted garlic and a cheese such as telemé or Parmesan. Brining gives a result that is twice as good as not brining: The meat tastes slightly sweet, the flavor is deeper, and the meat is more tender. Use the brine for any cut of beef, poultry, game, or even soft-fleshed white fish such as cod or halibut. If you want to double the recipe, you do not need to double the brine.

FOR THE BRINE: Bring the brine ingredients to a boil over high heat in a large pot. Stir and simmer 3 minutes.

Put short ribs in brine and weight down with a plate so ribs are submerged. Let sit, refrigerated, up to 4 hours. Remove meat and pat dry with paper towels.

FOR THE RIBS: Preheat oven to 350 degrees F. Heat olive oil in a large nonreactive sauté pan over medium-high heat until oil is almost smoking. Add meat, lower heat to medium, and brown on all sides, about 10 minutes. Remove ribs to a plate as they brown. Pour off all but 2 tablespoons fat and return pan to heat.

Add onion, celery, and carrot and sauté until vegetables are browned, about 10 minutes. Make sure to scrape up any browned bits from the bottom and sides of the pan. Season with salt and pepper to taste. Add vinegar and wine and bring to a boil over high heat. Boil until reduced by half. Add stock and bring to a boil again. Add ribs, scatter tomatoes over meat, cover, and braise in the preheated oven until meat is tender, about 3 hours.

When done, remove from oven and let rest, covered, 30 minutes. The meat will reabsorb cooking liquid as it cools. Remove ribs to a platter. Pour braising liquid into a narrow bowl and skim off fat, then bring to a boil in a sauté pan and cook until reduced to a sauce consistency.

To serve, reheat meat in braising liquid. Boil to reduce to a sauce consistency if necessary. Whisk in oregano and adjust salt and pepper. Garnish with parsley.

Chef's Notes

It is important to let the brine cool before adding meat, fish, or poultry. If you do not brine the meat, season it well with salt and pepper before browning. Cross-cut ribs are large, and the meat texture is dense because the cut is across the grain of the meat and the bone. They are an even size, end to end, so they soak up brine and cook at an even rate. English-cut short ribs are cut along the lengths of the bone. The meat tapers in thickness down toward each end and the grain is looser since it runs parallel with the bone. These short ribs will work very well as a substitute but cut the brining time to about 3 hours.

BASIC BRINE FOR BEEF AND POULTRY

10 cups water

2 cups kosher salt

2 cups packed dark brown sugar

10 juniper berries (optional)

2 bay leaves

SHORT RIBS

4 three-bone, cross-cut beef short ribs, 1 pound each (see Chef's Notes)

¼ cup extra-virgin olive oil

1 large onion, cut into ½-inch dice

1 stalk celery, cut into ½-inch dice

1 medium carrot, cut into ½-inch dice

Salt and freshly ground pepper

½ cup red wine vinegar or apple cider vinegar

1 cup dry red wine

3 cups chicken stock (page 42) or low-salt, canned chicken broth

2 medium vine-ripe tomatoes, peeled, seeded, and chopped

1 tablespoon finely chopped fresh oregano

1 tablespoon finely chopped fresh flat-leaf parsley

13 HERBAL VINEGAR

Vinegar flavored with herbs is hardly a new idea. Gardeners and cooks have been making them for centuries. For me, however, the problem with commercial herb vinegar is often a lack of flavor, while the problem with my garden is often too many herbs. If you, like me, are an enthusiastic grower of herbs, your tarragon grows to three feet high and so does the oregano. The question is always: What to do with it all?

Using the bounty to make strongly flavored herb vinegar is as good an answer as I can think of. The technique I use is a simple, quick purée of herbs and vinegar that is immediately strained to give a fresh and delightfully flavorful result. You can use up all your excess herbs and produce a huge flavor that you can thin out with more vinegar if you choose. Having too much flavor is not the problem; having not enough flavor is.

To use my technique, you do not have to think way ahead but can take inspiration from the moment—from whatever is at the market or in the garden. In fact, I would advise making only small batches of vinegar so that its flavor is as fresh as possible. Rose petals, lemon verbena, and sage will each make wonderful vinegar. You might try complementary flavors—blends of fruit and herb vinegar, for instance, or sage added to raspberry and basil to mango. Or use several herbs to mix into a tomato-garlic vinegar to create a Mediterranean-inspired blend. Only be sure your herbs, vegetables, and flowers, especially, are not sprayed with any pesticides!

Various herbal vinegars are wonderful additions to the pantry if only because we eat so many salads these days. Making vinaigrette with a different vinegar each time can vary the flavor without having to create a whole new recipe. Herbal vinegar can also perk up and add new flavors to all sorts of sauces and soups, especially tomato- and bean-based preparations.

The one herb I would not recommend infusing is thyme. I use a good deal of thyme in my cooking and always use the fresh herb. Its flavor is not appealing to me either dried or infused in vinegar or oil. I recommend growing thyme in your garden or in a pot in a sunny location, even if you grow no other herbs. Luckily, fresh herbs are becoming more common in supermarkets and, because thyme is so widely used, it should be available fresh year-round.

Make herbal vinegars with good-quality champagne vinegar. The flavor of red wine vinegar will mask that of most herbs. Rosemary, however, makes a very good flavored red wine vinegar. Use red wine vinegar to make assertive spice vinegars or lively blends of herbs and spices such as bay, garlic, black pepper, and rosemary. How much of each ingredient you use to flavor the vinegar depends on your taste as well as the quality of the ingredients to be infused. Start with more rather than less and search for the most flavorful herbs and freshest spices you can find. If the result is too strong, add unflavored vinegar until you have a balance you like.

If you want to infuse spices such as peppercorns, coriander, juniper, and the like, heat the vinegar to just under boiling. Add spices and let sit until cool. Do not strain out spices before bottling. To make an interesting chili vinegar, infuse peppercorns and dried chilies in hot vinegar, then bottle with chopped fresh hot and sweet peppers.

Use herbal vinegars in any recipe calling for white wine vinegar or champagne vinegar. The herbal flavor will increase the complexity of the dish.

As with all vinegars, use nonreactive cookware when heating them, store them in glass containers, and do not use metallic caps or lids to cover them.

# HERBAL VINEGAR

1 cup fresh green herb leaves, tightly packed (such as basil, tarragon, lavender flowers and leaves, oregano, mint, sage, chives)

1 cup champagne vinegar (6 percent acidity)

Pinch salt

This is an incredibly simple, fast process that gives a fresh herb flavor. Your basic vinegar takes on just a tinge of color, which, however, is not stable: The fresh, light green begins to oxidize in a few minutes and takes on a slight brownish cast in comparison to when first made. For the most spectacular presentation, make the vinegar just before use. The flavor does not change even if the color does. Add a leaf or two of the fresh herb to the bottle when bottling to help with identification.

I use vinegar with six percent acidity for these herbal vinegars, the standard strength of many imported vinegars. The American vinegar standard is usually five percent. If you use a stronger vinegar, increase the amount of fresh herbs. When you use your herbal vinegar in other recipes, you will have to taste as you go and adjust for a balance that suits your palate.

I suggest straining herb vinegar through a fine mesh sieve. If you want a very clear vinegar, you can filter it through rinsed and squeezed-dry coffee filters. However, you will also be filtering out flavor.

A very pretty touch is to add the herb flowers to the vinegar once it is strained, especially chive blossoms, separated into florets. These have a wonderful, zesty bite to them and it is a shame to see them dry and unpicked on the plant.

Put herbs, vinegar, and salt in a blender and blend on high speed about 30 seconds. Strain through a fine strainer into a clean glass bottle. Press on the solids to extract all the vinegar and flavor. Use immediately when it is a fresh, frothy, delicate green. The color will oxidize right before your eyes, turning darker green with a brownish hue. The flavor, however, is stable. Store the vinegar in a cool, dark place, tightly covered with a nonmetallic lid.

VARIATION FOR ROSEMARY VINEGAR: Use ½ cup rosemary sprigs to 1 cup vinegar. Also, in winter or under drought conditions, rosemary will get very tough and resinous. If this is the shape your rosemary is in, blanch it first for about 30 seconds in boiling water. It is not necessary to plunge it in ice water afterwards; just put it straight into the blender with the vinegar.

Chef's Notes

Opal basil keeps its lovely opal color and allows you surprising presentation possibilities.

TOD'S COLESLAW

Serves 6 to 8

1 head (about 2 pounds) white cabbage, finely shredded

¾ cup finely sliced red onion

1 cup sugar

1 cup herbal vinegar (page 171) or apple cider vinegar

¾ cup vegetable oil or corn oil

1 tablespoon whole celery seed

1 teaspoon salt

Todney Stoner, sous chef of our restaurant, Ajax Tavern, in Aspen, Colorado, gave me his mother's family recipe for coleslaw. His family is from West Virginia and the salad is one of the most amazingly good-tasting slaws I have ever had. It is awesome on a barbecued piece of brisket. Tod makes it every day for the restaurant, varying it occasionally by adding other vegetables such as carrot and radicchio.

Layer ⅓ of the cabbage and onion in a nonreactive bowl. Sprinkle with ¼ cup sugar. Repeat twice and let sit 15 to 20 minutes at room temperature.

Combine remaining ¼ cup sugar with vinegar, oil, celery seed, and salt in a nonreactive saucepan and bring to a boil over high heat. Stir until sugar is dissolved. Immediately pour over the cabbage and onion and mix well. Cover with plastic wrap and weight down with cans or even with a stack of plates. Refrigerate 24 hours before serving.

VARIATION WITH RED CABBAGE: Red cabbage makes a pretty slaw. Do not try a mix of green and red; the red color bleeds and colors the whole batch.

POACHED EGG AND PROSCIUTTO BRUSCHETTA

Serves 4

4 long slices crusty, country bread, cut about ½ inch thick

2 tablespoons flavored olive oil such as roasted garlic or basil olive oil (see page 182)

8 thin slices (about 1½ ounces total) prosciutto

4 cups water

¾ cup (about) herbal vinegar (page 171), such as basil or chive

8 eggs

2-3 cups mixed salad greens

Salt and freshly ground pepper

This makes a great brunch, lunch, or late supper dish—very easy to cook and full of satisfying flavors and textures. Though it may seem strange to dress greens with vinegar alone and to drizzle the cooked eggs with more vinegar, trust me! The acidity cuts the sometimes heavy, fat flavor of egg yolk and leaves the palate refreshed.

Lightly brush bread on one side with oil and toast on both sides. Cut each piece in half on the diagonal and put 2 halves (oiled side up) on each of 4 hot plates. Arrange a slice of prosciutto on top of each half. Keep warm.

Bring 4 cups water and ½ cup herbal vinegar to a boil in a wide nonreactive saucepan but make sure water is at least 1½ inches deep. Poach eggs by cracking them and then slipping them gently into the water. Use a spoon to hold the whites close to the yolk. Poach just a few at a time and cook just until whites are set and yolks are still runny, about 1½ minutes. Remove and drain on paper towels.

Season greens with salt and pepper and a splash of vinegar. Arrange a handful on each plate, then top each piece of toast with an egg and season with salt and pepper. Drizzle or spray a little more vinegar over the eggs and serve.

MIGNONETTE
WITH JET COLD OYSTERS

1 shallot, finely minced

3 tablespoons herbal vinegar (page 171) flavored with tarragon

Salt and freshly ground pepper

1 teaspoon finely chopped fresh flat-leaf parsley

24 fresh oysters on the half shell (see Chef's Notes)

Here in northern California we are lucky to have terrific oyster farmers. Many people make an outing of driving to Bodega Bay or Inverness in order to stop for oysters and see the ocean. The oystermen also often come inland to our farmers' markets. Oysters can close their shells so tightly that they remain alive, if kept cold, even if out of the water for several days. This simple, traditional sauce for oysters is a wonderful way to showcase freshly made herbal vinegar. Make sure your pepper is freshly cracked. The flavor of the course bits of pepper are a great foil for the sweet saltiness of the oysters. Have twenty-four oysters for four romantic people.

In a small bowl, mix together shallot, vinegar, and salt and pepper to taste. Add parsley just before serving. The parsley helps the mignonette adhere to the oysters. Arrange oysters, still on their half shells, on a bed of ice and spoon mignonette over them.

Chef's Notes

When you buy your oysters, buy them as fresh as possible. Ask the oysterman or fishmonger how old the oysters are. Do not buy them if they are more than three days old. Also, have the fishmonger shuck the oysters for you, leaving them on the half shell and catching the oyster liquor in the take-home container.

WARM PASTA VEGETABLE SALAD

Serves 4 to 6

1 pound broccoli

5 tablespoons extra-virgin
olive oil

2 tablespoons finely
chopped garlic

¼ teaspoon New Mexican red
pepper flakes (see page 183)

1 tablespoon finely chopped
fresh thyme

Salt and freshly ground pepper

2 cups chicken stock
(page 42) or low-salt,
canned chicken broth

1 pound zucchini, sliced into
¼-inch-thick rounds (if large,
cut zucchini in half first)

3 tablespoons herbal
vinegar (page 171) flavored
with oregano

2 medium tomatoes,
cut into large chunks

2 tablespoons finely chopped
fresh flat-leaf parsley

1 pound dried fusilli pasta

½ cup freshly grated Parmesan
cheese

I find it nearly impossible to get flavor in cold pasta salads; the starch seems to hide all my flavor efforts. This warm pasta salad has a clean, light taste. The sauce is a pan vinaigrette. It and the vegetables may be done ahead of time, but the pasta should be cooked at the last minute so it is hot when mixed with the vinaigrette. The dish is then served warm or at room temperature. Feel free to use any vegetables you like—for instance, asparagus and roasted red bell peppers—taking advantage of seasonal produce.

Separate broccoli into florets. Peel stems down to the light green, tender core, then slice into thin rounds on the diagonal. Keep florets and stems separate.

Heat 2 tablespoons oil in a sauté pan until almost smoking. Add garlic and sauté until light brown, moving the pan off and on heat to regulate temperature. Add red pepper flakes and thyme. Stir. Add broccoli florets and sauté about 1 minute. Season with salt and pepper.

Add chicken stock to sauté pan and bring to a boil. Cook until broccoli is half cooked, about 3 minutes. Add broccoli stems and zucchini and cook until tender, about another 3 minutes. Scoop out vegetables with a strainer and spread on a baking sheet to cool.

Bring cooking liquid to a boil and boil until it is thick and saucelike. You should have about ½ cup. Add vinegar, stir, then add tomatoes and stir just so they warm but do not cook. Season to taste with salt and pepper. Add remaining olive oil and parsley. Mix well.

Meanwhile, bring a large pot of salted water to a boil. Cook pasta until al dente, drain, pour into a serving bowl, and immediately toss with pan vinaigrette, vegetables, and half the cheese. Sprinkle with remaining cheese and serve warm.

BRAISED LEEK AND POTATO SALAD

Serves 4

This is not a California Cuisine salad! When I braise vegetables, I like them to be meltingly tender at the finish. This is when their flavor is the sweetest. I have created a fun presentation for a very earthy salad but since taste is more important, feel free to cut the vegetables into bite-size pieces and toss with the dressing in a serving bowl. The tops and trimmings from the leeks may be fried for a garnish or saved for making soup.

Put unpeeled potatoes in a pot of salted, cold water and bring to a boil. Simmer until tender, about 15 minutes. Do not overcook. Drain, let cool, and cut into ⅜-inch-thick slices. Keep slices in order so potatoes may be reassembled.

Preheat oven to 350 degrees F. Cut off and discard all but 5 or 6 inches of white parts of leeks. Melt butter with bay leaf in an ovenproof skillet over medium-high heat. Add white parts of leeks and toss to coat well with butter. Add thyme and season with salt and pepper. Add chicken stock and bring to a boil. Cover and cook in the preheated oven until very tender, about 10 minutes. When done, drain leeks and let cool on a plate. Remove and discard bay leaf from skillet, but do not discard cooking liquid. Cut leeks lengthwise into halves or quarters, if necessary. Season again with salt and pepper.

Place skillet with cooking liquid over medium-high heat. Bring to a boil and boil until reduced to a sauce consistency, about ¼ cup. Remove from heat and immediately whisk in 1½ tablespoons vinegar. Add parsley. Slowly add olive oil while whisking to form an emulsion. Taste for balance and add more vinegar if necessary.

Arrange about 3 pieces of leek on each of 4 plates. Drizzle with pan vinaigrette. Lay potato slices out in order, season with salt and pepper, and drizzle with vinaigrette. Turn over and repeat on the second side. Stack potato slices on each plate to reassemble one potato per person. Drizzle with more vinaigrette and sprinkle with chives. Garnish the top with a small handful of fried leeks, if desired.

4 medium potatoes
(about 1 pound),
such as Yukon Gold
or red potatoes

1 pound trimmed leeks
(about ¾ inch in diameter or
larger leeks cut in half)

2 tablespoons unsalted butter

1 bay leaf

1 tablespoon finely chopped
fresh thyme

Salt and freshly ground pepper

1 cup chicken stock
(page 42) or low-salt,
canned chicken broth

2 tablespoons herbal vinegar
(page 171), flavored with chives

1 tablespoon finely chopped
fresh flat-leaf parsley

2 tablespoons extra-virgin
olive oil

1 tablespoon finely chopped
fresh chives

Fried julienne of leek
(optional) (see Chef's Notes)

Chef's Notes

Fried leek tops are delicious and a good use of some of the leek tops that might otherwise be thrown away. They make a nice complement to fish dishes as well as this salad. Cut the pale yellow-green inner leaves lengthwise into strips as fine as you can manage. Dip in buttermilk, drain, then toss with arborio rice flour coating (page 154). Deep-fry in 375 degrees F oil until crispy and a pale gold. It is important to start potatoes cooking in cold water so they will cook evenly throughout.

TOMATO AND GORGONZOLA SALAD WITH CRISPY ONION RINGS

Serves 4

The cheese and onion rings provide enough fat so that a vinaigrette with oil is unnecessary. I do recommend buying a deep-fat fryer if you like to make fried foods with any regularity. The fryer keeps temperatures even and, because the heating coils are on the sides as opposed to the bottom, the solids that always fall to the bottom of the pan will not burn and spoil the flavor of the oil and the food you are preparing.

In a deep-fat fryer or large heavy saucepan, heat oil to 375 degrees F (see Chef's Notes). Preheat oven to 200 degrees F. Place onions in a nonreactive bowl and pour buttermilk over them. Toss well. Place onions in a strainer to drain well, then dust with rice flour coating. Shake off excess over a plate or waxed paper. Deep-fry until golden brown, about 2 minutes. Do not touch the onions too often or you will rip the coating. Keep them separate and try to keep them under the surface of the fat so they brown evenly. The first batch will cook more quickly than the remainder. Drain on paper towels, sprinkle with salt, and place in oven to keep warm. Onions can be made ahead and kept warm; this coating does not get soggy.

Cut a slice off the top and bottom of each tomato (do not core) and cut in half horizontally. Arrange tomatoes on a platter or 2 slices on each of 4 plates. Season with salt and pepper and sprinkle with cheese and vinegar. Top each salad with about 3 overlapping onion rings and serve.

4 cups peanut oil for deep-frying

1 red onion, sliced ⅜ inch thick and separated into rings (see Chef's Notes)

½ cup buttermilk

½ cup seasoned Arborio Rice Flour Coating (page 154)

Salt and freshly ground pepper

2 pounds (about 4 large) vine-ripe tomatoes

⅓ cup finely crumbled Gorgonzola or other blue-veined cheese or freshly grated Parmesan cheese

2 tablespoons herbal vinegar (page 171), flavored with basil or oregano

Chef's Notes

Use the larger, outer rings for this dish and save the smaller, inner rings for another purpose. You want the onion to cook quickly and to get brown and crisp without burning (temperature is too hot) and without getting soggy (temperature is too low). If, however, you have neither deep-fryer nor thermometer, heat your oil over medium-high heat until you can see it begin to swirl. Begin to test the temperature by dropping in a single piece of food, such as a frozen French fry. The oil will be hot enough when it actively bubbles as soon as the potato is put in and the potato browns crisply within about 1 minute. Make sure to bring the oil temperature back up to the correct heat between batches.

GLOSSARY and BUYING GUIDE

AL DENTE:

An Italian term meaning to the tooth, used to describe the correct texture of well-cooked risotto and pasta. The rice or pasta should give some resistance when bitten into. When the grain or pasta is cut, there should be no trace of whiteness inside. Instead it should have a consistent color.

ARBORIO RICE FLOUR:

My staff and I worked a long time to find a perfect coating for fried foods. One day we tested every flour we had, in every combination. It occurred to me to use the rice powder mixed with flour as a coating for fried foods. Rice has a higher sugar content than wheat so it would brown more quickly in the fryer. The seafood would not overcook before the coating browned. In addition, the slightly grainy texture of the rice flour makes the coating attractive to the eye as well as the tooth and, even better, it does not get soggy! This allows the cook to make the fried food ahead of time and keep it warm in a low oven. However, you can use any white rice. You will need to blend at least a cup at a time. Place rice in blender and blend until you have tiny granules about the texture of powdered gelatin. One cup rice yields a little less than 1 1/4 cups rice flour. For my rice flour coating for deep-frying, see page 154.

ARUGULA:

An herb or salad green also known as rocket and roquette. It should be gathered when young and tender and the leaves are an even medium green. It will dehydrate and go limp quickly on a store shelf if not properly stored. Only buy fresh, bright-looking bunches. When young, arugula has a delicious peppery flavor, good as a salad on its own or mixed with other salad greens. When it gets older, we call it cowboy arugula because the pepper flavor intensifies and gets almost hot. That is the time to add it to a dish such as pasta at the last moment so the arugula just wilts.

If you grow arugula in your garden, reseed it every three to four weeks to ensure a constant supply of young leaves. Plant it in a part of the garden that is shady: the hotter the weather, the hotter the flavor. The plants, if trimmed back, will grow new leaves, but this technique also tends to increase the herb's bitterness. Watercress and baby spinach can both be substituted for arugula.

BALSAMIC VINEGAR:

A rich, full-bodied vinegar, dark in color with some natural sweetness. Originally from Modena, Italy, and very expensive because of its production techniques and twelve-year aging, the vinegar is now mass produced and short-cuts are taken to produce a similar flavor to the original. The less-expensive brands work very well in cooking; however, it is always a good idea to taste your bottle to familiarize yourself with its characteristics.

BRUSCHETTA:

Traditionally, bruschetta are slices of rustic bread grilled outdoors and drizzled with good olive oil. Topped with mozzarella, chicken livers, or mushrooms, they are often served as part of an antipasto.

CALIFORNIA CHILI POWDER:

This is not like the chili powder found in the spice section of grocery stores. Those are most commonly a blend of powdered chilies, cumin, and oregano. California chili powder is finely ground, whole, dried California chilies with nothing added. California chilies are only mildly hot. You can find whole and ground California chilies in well-stocked Mexican groceries. Two brands are Mojave Foods (6200 E. Slauson Avenue, City of Commerce, CA 90040) and El Guapo (631 S. Anderson Street, Los Angeles, CA 90023). Also look for various types of dried chilies at your farmers' market. Tierra Vegetables grows many varieties of chilies without pesticides, herbicides, or fumigants. You can mail order their dried chilies. Write to them at 13684 Chalk Hill Road, Healdsburg, CA 95448; 707-433-5666.

CANNELLONI BEANS:

White, oval beans, usually smallish, but I like mine large, at least ½ inch long. Bigger beans seem to have more flavor as well as having a higher flesh-to-skin ratio, and skins can be hard to digest. If your dried beans are old, toss them out. Old beans take much longer to cook than those from a more recent harvest. I do not consider canned beans an adequate substitute; to me, they have no texture.

A great source for top-quality, large cannelloni beans (as well as a large variety of other organic herbs, vegetables, and dried beans) is Phipps Ranch, P.O. Box 349, 2700 Pescadero Road, Pescadero, CA 94060. Call 415-879-0787 for a catalog or write. Mail order, retail, and wholesale.

CAPERS:

The flower buds of a bush native to tropical and subtropical areas. In the current fashion of cutting down on salt, it is a good idea to rinse the brine from capers and then drain. If capers are large, roughly chop them before adding to a recipe; otherwise, use them whole.

FLAT-LEAF PARSLEY:

Also called Italian parsley. It is a variety of the common curly-leafed parsley but has dark green, flat leaves and a good, strong parsley flavor. Flat-leaf parsley is widely available in supermarkets, and the curly-leafed parsley is not an adequate substitute. The parsley does grow easily in the garden from seed without bolting or going to seed too quickly. The herb can be used, when young and tender, as a vegetable on its own, as a salad with a mustard vinaigrette and freshly grated Parmesan cheese, and as a pasta topping chopped fine and added to hot pasta with roasted garlic oil. As long as there is a bunch of parsley and flavored oils in the refrigerator, it is possible to make a great meal.

FLAVORED OLIVE OIL:

Flavored oils are easily made by briefly puréeing a large amount of fresh herbs (such as basil) with a small amount of oil, filtering the result, and thinning with more olive oil. The oil should not be an extra-virgin olive oil. It has too distinct a taste of its own and will compete with the flavor you want to add to the oil. To infuse spices such as cinnamon and peppercorns, fried chilies, dried, wild mushrooms, and resinous herbs such as rosemary, heat the flavoring and oil together very gently for less than a minute, then filter.

Again use a large amount of spice and a small amount of oil (1 cup minimum to make it worth your while). If the flavor is too strong, just add more oil to achieve the balance you prefer.

Roasted garlic oil, one of the most popular oils and a wonderful oil with many applications at the stove (I use it to sauté all sorts of vegetables, to add to salad dressing, and the like), is the by-product of making roasted garlic. Or roasted garlic is the by-product of roasted garlic oil! Roast six to eight large heads of fresh garlic seasoned with salt and pepper in a cup or two of olive oil until tender, very soft, and caramelized. Use the paste to spread on toast or sandwiches, to stir into soup, and so forth, and bottle the oil.

Flavored oils will keep, refrigerated, for a week. I recommend making small batches with the most flavorful herbs and spices you can find. Taste the oil you plan to use as well to make sure it has a pleasantly neutral flavor. If you do not have the flavored oil called for in a recipe, go ahead and make it anyway. Use extra-virgin olive oil and, if you have it, the fresh herb.

For food safety reasons, it is important to make only small batches of flavored oils, keep them refrigerated, and use them quickly, within a week. If you choose to make garlic oil, soak the raw cloves in distilled vinegar for 30 minutes, then rinse with water, drain, and pulse in a blender with a little oil. Press the oil out of the solids, discard solids, and add more oil to the flavored oil until you have a flavor balance to suit your palate.

KOSHER SALT:

I use only kosher salt in my cooking. I like the fact that it is pure salt. The table salt label in front of me lists calcium silicate, dextrose, and potassium iodide as well as salt. Kosher salt is also less expensive than sea salt. If you want to use the best salt I know of, look in specialty markets for gray salt, an unprocessed sea salt from Brittany, France. If you do not have, or cannot find, kosher salt, use table salt but in lower amounts than my recipes specify.

NEW MEXICAN CHILI FLAKES/ RED PEPPER FLAKES:

Chilies vary in heat from brand to brand. Shop until you find a brand you like, then stick with it. New Mexican chilies are medium hot. You can substitute the crushed red pepper flakes you find easily in the supermarket, but you may want to cut back on the amount called for in my recipe. You can find New Mexican chilies in well-stocked Mexican groceries. Buy the whole, dried chilies and grind them coarsely. Store in a tightly sealed jar.

OLIVE PASTE:

Olive paste is simply very finely chopped and pitted olives. It can be made from green olives though it is more commonly made from black olives. Brined olives such as kalamata give the paste a different flavor than intense, oil-cured olives. Black olive paste (usually flavored with anchovy and capers) is the base for tapenade, a typical Provençal spread served on toast as an appetizer.

ORECCHIETTI:

Little ears in Italian. A circular, shallow, bowl-shaped pasta about ¼ inch in diameter. Its shape catches and holds pasta sauces; it is often served with meat sauces.

PANCETTA:

Commonly referred to as Italian bacon. It is cured pork belly but not smoked as is American bacon. American bacon may be substituted and will add a smoky flavor to the dish. Pancetta is sold in flat pieces or rolled into rounds. Used as a flavoring for soups and sauces.

PAPPARDELLE:

Egg noodles similar to tagliatelle and fettuccine but cut much wider, about 1 inch.

PARMESAN CHEESE:

A hard, cow's milk cheese made in the Parma region of Emilia in central Italy. It is made only during the spring, summer, and early fall when the cows eat fresh grass. The rind forms naturally during aging. The best are aged two years before sale, but Parmesan is now being imported much younger, six to eight months old. The cheese will then have a milder taste and softer texture.

Members of the Parmesan producers association stamp each of their cheeses on the rind with the cheese's name. To identify the real thing, look on the rind for the words (or what part you can read on the cut pieces) parmigiano-reggiano. Cheeses made outside of the small area restricted for Parmesan production and cheeses made during the winter when cows eat dry hay are called grana. These are very acceptable substitutes for Parmesan and are sometimes preferable when the dominant flavor of very aged Parmesan would detract from the effect of the entire dish. Parmesan and especially pecorino (see next page) have very high sodium contents. When a recipe calls for Parmesan, undersalt to compensate and add the cheese before the final adjustment of seasoning. When heating the cheese, do so only until it softens or turns a pale gold. If it becomes overly brown it will taste bitter. Save the rind

and put it whole or cut into small pieces in soups to flavor them. The rind will soften and taste delicious.

There is not yet a domestic version of Parmesan I would use, but some good versions are made in Argentina, for instance. If you must buy grated cheese, buy that which the store has grated that day and keep it in the freezer.

PASTEURIZED LIQUID EGGS AND CHOLESTEROL-FREE LIQUID EGGS:

Because of the dual threats of salmonella and cholesterol, many people have become concerned about using raw eggs and even under-cooked eggs with runny yolks such as poached or coddled eggs. The most important thing to remember is to buy fresh eggs that have been refrigerated and to refrigerate them as soon as you get home. Use them directly from the refrigerator or leave at room temperature for no more than a few hours. The California Egg Commission (1150 North Mountain Avenue, Suite 114, Upland, CA 91786, 909-981-4923) has very good information available. Recently, pasteurized eggs have begun to be available to consumers. For many years bakeries and restaurants have been using pasteurized liquid eggs—whole eggs with the shells. The FDA requires that these products be pasteurized. While commercial establishments may buy pasteurized egg yolks, egg whites, or whole eggs, consumers, at the moment, can only purchase pasteurized whole eggs. They are packaged in cartons and sold in the refrigerated section of the supermarket. One brand in California is called Nulaid. Follow directions on the package and use the equivalent of 1 whole egg for the mayonnaise recipes in this book. Cholesterol-free liquid eggs are readily available and work for these recipes as well. Use ¼ cup liquid egg and 1 tablespoon vinegar or lemon juice and proceed with the recipe as written. The texture is very light but the emulsion does not break and it tastes very good. There is the added benefit of enjoying mayonnaise without fear of cholesterol!

PASTINA:

A tiny, pellet-shaped, dried pasta traditionally used in soups. It is sold by De Cecco as #78 Acini de Pepe.

PECORINO CHEESE:

As normally sold in the United States, pecorino is an aged Italian sheep's milk cheese meant for grating. It is used for many of the same purposes as Parmesan though it has a sharper, saltier flavor. There are domestic versions of pecorino as well as imports from countries other than Italy. To find the one you like best, buy small pieces to taste and compare.

POLENTA:

Polenta (the dried ground kernels of corn) is a New World food introduced to Europe by explorers who reached the Americas. It fit well into the peasant style of cooking throughout Italy. Peasant cuisines usually include a cooked grain mush as a staple of the diet. The grain would be whatever grew well in that region. It is the Italians, however, who made an inspired dish of simple cornmeal mush. The word *polenta* is used for both the grain—coarsely ground, yellow cornmeal—and the dish it makes when cooked with water or other liquid into a stiff paste.

PORCINI MUSHROOMS:

To an Italian, the porcini (a variety of boletus) is king of the mushroom family. They have a wonderful, aromatic, rich, gamy scent and flavor. Usually sold dried in ½-ounce or 1-ounce packages, porcini can occasionally be found fresh. Italians grill a whole, large porcini and serve it with garlic and herbs as a first course. Rehydrate porcini and other dried mushrooms by placing them in a bowl and pouring boiling water over them. To keep them under the surface of the water, press a paper towel down into the bowl or simply stir them occasionally. Let sit until soft, about 15 minutes. Squeeze out water over bowl and prepare as called for in the recipe. Use the water to flavor soups, stocks, sauces, etc.

RED PEPPER FLAKES:

Also called chili flakes but distinct from the chili powder blends sold in stores for making chili. I use New Mexico chili flakes. To make them at home and guarantee their heat, buy whole, dried hot chilies and grind them in a spice mill or coffee grinder reserved for grinding spices. Store in a tightly sealed jar. To toast red pepper flakes, add to hot olive oil in a sauté pan and heat just until flakes begin to move and sizzle. If not using oil, add to a hot, dry pan and immediately remove from the heat. Be sure to have your stove fan on and do not breathe the aroma—it sears your lungs! Scrape flakes onto a dish as soon as they become fragrant and slightly brown.

ROASTING RED BELL PEPPERS AND CHILI PEPPERS:

Roast the peppers under a preheated broiler or over an open flame or grill, turning them occasionally until skins are charred all over. Place in a bowl, cover with a lid, and let steam to loosen the skins. When cool enough to handle, peel off the charred skins. Remove and discard core, seeds, and veins. This is most easily done standing at the sink but do not rinse peppers under water! You will wash away half their flavor. Catch juices by working over the bowl. Tear or cut peppers into strips and put in a bowl. Pour cooking liquids over, straining out the seeds. Cover and refrigerate up to 2 days. When handling chili peppers, take care not to burn your skin. Wear gloves, do not touch sensitive parts of your face (especially your eyes), and wash hands immediately afterward.

SEMOLINA:

Semolina is produced by milling durum wheat, a hard, winter wheat. After the bran is removed and before the grains are ground into flour, large particles of the endosperm are separated out and sold separately as semolina. It is pale yellow and has a coarse texture. Semolina is used in puddings, as a thickener in soups, and to make pasta. It can be purchased in Italian food markets.

SHIITAKE MUSHROOMS:

Asian mushrooms sold fresh and dried (sold as black forest mushrooms in Chinese markets). They have a rich, meaty flavor which makes them a welcome addition to an entrée vegetarian dish and allows them to substitute well for wild mushrooms. Shiitakes are now cultivated in the United States by a number of producers and thus are more readily available in the fresh vegetable section of well-stocked stores. Soak the dried mushrooms in warm water to cover (press several paper towels down on mushrooms to submerge them) 15 minutes. Squeeze mushrooms over bowl to catch the liquid, then cut off and discard stems. Slice or chop caps and cook. Strain the mushroom soaking liquid and add to your dish to give the flavor a boost.

TOASTED PINE NUTS, PISTACHIOS, AND OTHER NUTS:

Preheat oven to 350 degrees F. Scatter nuts on a baking pan and place in oven until lightly browned. Stir occasionally so they brown evenly. Pine nuts should take no longer than 3 to 5 minutes and burn easily, so keep your eye on them! Pistachios take about 5 minutes; walnuts, hazelnuts, and pecans take about 10 minutes. A toaster oven works very well for this small job. You might want to toast a larger amount than any recipe calls for, then store the extra toasted nuts in a glass jar in the freezer.

TOMATOES, CANNED:

Nothing substitutes for vine-ripened tomatoes from the garden. But in the off season when I get hungry for tomato sauce, I use canned tomatoes. It is a good idea to buy several brands of canned tomatoes and taste them to see which you like best since their sweetness and acidity will vary. In the recipes I have called for plum (Roma) tomatoes though I did some testing with the supermarket brand S&W Red Pack. The results were excellent.

VINEGAR-MAKING SUPPLIES:

The Cantinetta, a small delicatessen and take-out food shop across the stone courtyard from Tra Vigne, can outfit the new vinegar maker with whatever is needed: They carry a specially designed vinegar-making crock (it comes with a recipe for homemade vinegar) and active vinegar we made ourselves. You can write The Cantinetta at Tra Vigne, 1050 Charter Oak Road, St. Helena, CA 94574, or call 707-963-8888. Home winemaking shops are another good source for equipment and advice. One such shop is Oak Barrel Winecraft in Berkeley, CA (www.oakbarrel.com), and Napa Fermentation Supplies, P.O. Box 5839, Napa, CA 94581; 707-255-6372. They both have home vinegar making kits with barrels, instructions, and the active starter to get you going.

INDEX

TABLE of EQUIVALENTS

US/UK	METRIC
oz=ounce	g=gram
lb=pound	kg=kilogram
in=inch	mm=millimeter
ft=foot	cm=centimeter
tbl=tablespoon	ml=milliliter
fl oz=fluid ounce	l=liter
qt=quart	

The exact equivalents in the following tables have been rounded for convenience.

OVEN TEMPERATURES

Fahrenheit	Celsius	Gas
250	120	½
275	140	1
300	150	2
325	160	3
350	180	4
375	190	5
400	200	6
425	220	7
450	230	8
475	240	9
500	260	10

LIQUIDS

US	Metric	UK
2 tbl	30 ml	1 fl oz
¼ cup	30 ml	2 fl oz
⅓ cup	60 ml	3 fl oz
½ cup	80 ml	4 fl oz
⅔ cup	125 ml	5 fl oz
¾ cup	160 ml	6 fl oz
1 cup	180 ml	8 fl oz
1½ cups	250 ml	12 fl oz
2 cups	375 ml	16 fl oz
4 cups/1 qt	500 ml	32 fl oz

LENGTH MEASURES

⅛ in	3 mm
¼ in	6 mm
½ in	12 mm
1 in	2.5 cm
2 in	5 cm
3 in	7.5 cm
4 in	10 cm
5 in	13 cm
6 in	15 cm
7 in	18 cm
8 in	20 cm
9 in	23 cm
10 in	25 cm
11 in	28 cm
12 in/1 ft	30 cm

WEIGHTS

US/UK	Metric
1 oz	30 g
2 oz	60 g
3 oz	90 g
4 oz (¼ lb)	125 g
5 oz (⅓ lb)	155 g
6 oz	185 g
7 oz	220 g
8 oz (½ lb)	250 g
10 oz	315 g
12 oz (¾ lb)	375 g
14 oz	440 g
16 oz (1 lb)	500 g
1½ lb	750 g
2 lb	1 kg
3 lb	1.5 kg